Comparative Management Studies

Comparative Management Studies

Alan S. Gutterman

BUSINESS EXPERT PRESS

Comparative Management Studies

First published in 2019 by
Business Expert Press, LLC
222 East 46th Street, New York, NY 10017
www.businessexpertpress.com

ISBN-13: 978-1-94999-136-9 (paperback)
ISBN-13: 978-1-94999-137-6 (e-book)

Business Expert Press Human Resource Management and Organizational Behavior Collection

Collection ISSN: 1946-5637 (print)
Collection ISSN: 1946-5645 (electronic)

Cover and interior design by Exeter Premedia Services Private Ltd., Chennai, India

First edition: 2019

10 9 8 7 6 5 4 3 2 1

Printed in the United States of America.

Abstract

All managers, regardless of where they work, must understand certain basic concepts such as the functions, roles, and skills associated with the managerial position; the different levels of managerial effectiveness and how they are measured; and the styles available to managers and the factors that determine which style might be preferred in a particular instance. However, context matters and it is essential that managers understand the role that culture plays in being effective in their positions. This book begins with a brief description of the history and evolution of "management studies," a daunting topic given that it is generally recognized that economic and military activities have been raising issues of planning, directing, and control for thousands of years. The book continues with an overview of the scope and practice of comparative management studies and also describes the research that has been done on cross-cultural transfer of management theories, particularly attempts to transfer US management theories into other cultural contexts. In addition, the book includes materials on the search for, and analysis of, dimensions of management styles that can be used as a basis for creating models that can be used for comparison purposes. Among the dimensions of management styles discussed in the book are planning, organizing, staffing, leading, controlling, decision making, and motivating.

Keywords

management; cross-cultural management; management theories; comparative management; management in developing countries

Contents

CHAPTER 1

Introduction to Management Studies

Introduction

This chapter provides an introduction to the central and important topic of management studies. The study of management covers a wide array of topics such as organizational theory and behavior, strategic and human resources management, managerial functions and roles, and identification and training of management skills. The tools used by practitioners of management studies to collect and analyze information and disseminate findings within the research community and to practicing managers are similarly diverse. This chapter includes a brief description of the history and evolution of management studies, a daunting topic given that it is generally recognized that economic and military activities have been focusing on issues of planning, directing, and control for thousands of years and that one can find useful illustrations of management in the building of the pyramids in ancient Egypt, the operation of the complex trade routes during the Middle Ages, and the commercial activities of the wealthy family businesses throughout the Renaissance. Over the last few decades, hundreds of journals and periodicals devoted to management studies have been launched and management has become a mainstream topic as books by authors such as Peter Drucker and Tom Peters have climbed to the top of "best-seller" lists. The field of management education, taught as a distinct discipline in both universities and through commercial private sector initiatives, has been a fertile ground for textbooks.[1]

---

[1] Jones, G., and J. George. 2017. "There are a Number of Outstanding and Comprehensive Textbooks that Cover a Wide Range of Subjects Pertaining to "Management."" *Essentials of Contemporary Management*, 10th ed. New York, NY: McGraw-Hill Higher Education; Scott, J. 2013. *The Concise Handbook of*

Definitions of Management

Given that "management" has been so widely studied and practiced for literally thousands of years, it is not surprising to find a wide array of possible definitions of the term. At the most basic level, the verb "manage" derives from the Italian word "maneggiare," which is means "to handle." A number of definitions of "management" have focused on the specific tasks and activities that all managers, regardless of whether they are overseeing a business, a family or a social group, engage in, such as planning, organizing, directing, coordinating and controlling. One of the simplest, and often quoted, definitions of management was offered by Mary Parker Follett, who described it as "the art of getting things done through people."[2] The notion of "management through people" can also be found in the work of Weihrich and Koontz, who began with a basic definition of management as "the process of designing and maintaining an environment in which individuals, working together in groups, accomplish efficiently selected aims."[3] They then went on to expand this basic definition with the following observations:

- Managers carry out certain universally recognized basic managerial functions, including planning, organizing, staffing, leading and controlling.

Management: A Practitioner's Approach. London: Routledge; Schermerhorn, J. 2013. *Management*, 12th ed. New York, NY: Wiley; Griffin, R. 2016. *Management*, 12th ed. Boston, MA: Cengage Learning; Robbins, S., M. Coulter, and D. DeCenzo. 2010. *Fundamentals of Management*, 7th ed. Upper Saddle River, NJ: Prentice Hall: and Bateman, T.S., S. Snell, and R. Konopaske. 2016. *Management: Leading & Collaborating in a Competitive World*, 12th ed. New York, NY: McGraw-Hill Higher Education.

[2] Follett, M. 1942. "Dynamic Administration." In *Dynamic Administration: The Collected Papers of Mary Parker Follett*, eds. H. Metcalf and L. Urwick, New York, NY: Harper & Row.

[3] Weihrich, H., and H. Koontz. 1993. *Management: A Global Perspective*, 10th ed. New York, NY: McGraw-Hill. (as summarized in Weihrich, H. 2018. "Management: Science, Theory, and Practice." https://scribd.com/document/106629608/22550642-Management-Science-Theory-and-Practice (accessed December 31, 2018)).

- Management applies to any kind of organization.
- Management principles apply to managers at all levels of the organization, not just executives and senior managers positioned at the top of the organizational hierarchy.
- The goal of all managers is the same: to create a "surplus."
- Managers are concerned with improving productivity, which implies both effectiveness and efficiency.[4]

Elements mentioned by Weihrich and Koontz the aforementioned explanations and observations have figured prominently in other definitions of management. For example, Jones et al. referred to management as "the process of using an organization's resources to achieve specific goals through the functions of planning, organizing, leading and controlling."[5] The importance of managerial functions was also emphasized by Weihrich in his explanation of the "systems approach to organizational management" based on an "input–output" model in which "inputs" from an organization's external environment (i.e., people, capital, and technology) were transformed into "outputs" demanded by various organizational stakeholders in a transformation process based on and guided by managerial functions such as planning, organizing, staffing, leading, and controlling.[6]

Others infer that merely carrying out the functions typically associated with management is not sufficient and it is necessary to add certain other concepts such as "value creation," "wealth creation," "efficiency," and "productivity" to the equation. In fact, well-known management guru Peter Drucker proposed a definition of management that focused on "the process of administering and coordinating resources effectively, efficiently, and in an effort to achieve the goals of the organization."[7] In other

---

[4] Id.

[5] Jones, G., J. George, and C. Hill. 2000. *Contemporary Management*, 2nd ed. New York, NY: Irwin/McGraw-Hill.

[6] Weihrich, H. n.d. "Management: Science, Theory, and Practice." https://scribd.com/document/106629608/22550642-Management-Science-Theory-and-Practice (accessed December 31, 2018).

[7] Drucker, P. 1967. *The Effective Executive*. New York, NY: Harper & Row; and Drucker, P. June 2004. "What Makes an Effective Executive." *Harvard Business Review* 82, p. 58.

words, the efforts of managers need to be "effective," as demonstrated by the degree to which the goals of the organization are achieved, and they need to be "efficient," which is measured by productivity (i.e., generating a given output by using the fewest inputs, including capital and human resources).[8] In another one of his publications Drucker observed that with respect to economic and business activities "… management has failed if it fails to produce economic results. It has failed if it does not supply goods and services desired by the consumer at a price the consumer is willing to pay. It has failed if it does not improve or at least maintain the wealth producing capacity of the economic resources entrusted to it."[9] Therefore, in the business context, effective managers carry out a wide array of tasks and activities as they seek to combine capital, people, machines, equipment, and technology to produce goods and services that create profits and wealth for the owners of the business.

Management: Science, Art, or Both?

Weihrich has discussed the interesting question of whether management is best seen as a science or as art and has suggested that "[m]anaging, like so many other disciplines—medicine, music composition, engineering, accountancy, or even baseball—is in large measure an art but founded on a wealth of science."[10] He went on to caution that "[e]xecutives who attempt to manage without .... management science must trust to luck, intuition, or to past experience" and that managers seeking to avoid the tedious and dangerous path of learning through "trial and error" must be able to access the knowledge that has been accumulated

---

[8] Lewis, P., S. Goodman, P. Fandt, and J. Michlitsch. 2007. *Management: Challenges for Tomorrow's Leaders*, 5, 5th ed. Mason, OH: Thomson South-Western. (also quoting from Foust, D. December 20, 2004. "Gone Flat." *Business Week*, pp. 76–82 ("effectiveness means 'doing the right things' to achieve the appropriate goal, and efficiency means 'doing things right'")).

[9] Drucker, P. 1954. *The Practice of Management*. New York, NY: Harper & Row.

[10] Weihrich, H. n.d. "Management: Science, Theory, and Practice." https://scribd.com/document/106629608/22550642-Management-Science-Theory-and-Practice (accessed December 31, 2018).

regarding the practice of management.[11] Weihrich wrote that application of scientific methods to management, including determination of facts through observation followed by identification of causal relationships that can have value in predicting what might happen in similar circumstances, allows us to classify significant and pertinent management knowledge and derive certain principles that can be used as guidelines for managerial decisions and instructions. For example, a manager in a growing organization will eventually be confronted with the need to begin delegating authority and Weihrich suggests that the manager can turn to various principles of management that are relevant such as "the principle of delegating by results expected, the principle of equality of authority and responsibility, and the principle of unity of command." Principles are merely predictive; they do not guarantee a particular result. However, they do provide a tested starting point for the manager. Also important in the management field are "techniques," which Weihrich defined as "ways of doing things, methods for accomplishing a given result."[12] Like principles, techniques are originally based in theory and are tested to validate their effectiveness. Examples of management techniques listed by Weihrich include budgeting, cost accounting, networking planning and control techniques, managing-by-objectives and total quality management.

Management and Performance

As time has passed, management has come to be recognized as one of the core factors of production along with machines, materials, money, technology, and people. It is well-known that productivity has become a leading indicator of organizational performance and Drucker has argued that "[t]he greatest opportunity for increasing productivity is surely to be found in knowledge, work itself, and especially in management."[13] Bloom et al. coordinated a survey and analysis of more than 4,000 medium-sized manufacturing operations in Europe, the United States, and Asia and

---

[11] Id.

[12] Id.

[13] Drucker, P. 1973. *Management, Tasks, Responsibilities, Practices*, 69. New York, NY: Harper & Row, 1973.

their findings released in 2007 confirmed that "firms across the globe that apply accepted management practices well perform significantly better than those that do not."[14] Surveyed management practices included activities relating to shop floor operations, performance management and talent management, and performance metrics included labor productivity, sales growth, and return on capital employed. The United States led the way with respect to the quality of management among firms included in the survey; however, companies from other countries were gaining ground quickly and, in fact, at that time over 15% of the Indian and Chinese firms included in the survey were characterized as "better managed" than the average US firm.

Strong support for the importance of management practices in generating better firm performance was also found in an extensive survey by Bloom and Van Reenen involving firms in 17 countries.[15] Specifically, Bloom and Van Reenen confirmed that firms with "better" management practices tended to larger, more productive, grew faster, and had higher survival rates. Bloom and Ven Reenen also identified interesting differences between the surveyed countries with respect to management practices and they described their key findings as follows[16]:

- Management practices vary tremendously across firms and countries. Most of the difference in the average management score of a country was due to the size of the "long tail" of very badly managed firms. For example, relatively few US firms were very badly managed, while Brazil and India had many firms in that category.

---

[14] Bloom, N., S. Dorgan, J. Dowdy, and J. Van Reenen. 2018. "Management Practice & Productivity: Why they Matter." http://growingjobs.org/downloads/management_practice.pdf (accessed December 31, 2018). The surveyed companies were located in the United States, India, Italy, Germany, Portugal, Sweden, United Kingdom, Poland, France, Greece and China.

[15] Bloom, N., and J. Van Reenen. Winter 2010. "Why Do Management Practices Differ across Firms and Countries." *Journal of Economic Perspectives* 24, no. 1, pp. 203–24.

[16] Id. at 205.

- Countries and firms specialized in different styles of management. For example, firms in the United States scored much higher than firms in Sweden with respect to incentives; however, Swedish firms were stronger than US firms when it came to monitoring.
- Strong product market competition appeared to boost average management practices through a combination of eliminating the tail of badly managed firms and pushing incumbents to continuously improve their management practices.
- In general, multinationals were better managed regardless of the location of their headquarters office and were prone to transplanting their preferred management styles into their foreign subsidiaries. For example, subsidiaries of US multinationals operating in the UK were better at incentives and worse than monitoring than subsidiaries of Swedish multinationals also operating in the UK.
- Firms that exported into foreign markets but did not manufacture in foreign markets were better managed than those firms who stayed home and neither exported into or manufactured in foreign markets; however, firms that only exported were not as well managed as the multinationals who also manufactured in foreign markets.
- Family-owned firms that appointed a family member, such as the oldest son, to serve as the chief executive officer tended, on average, to be very badly managed.
- Government-owned firms tended to be extremely badly managed while publicly owned firms and firms owned by private equity investors were usually well managed.
- Firms that were more reliant on human capital, as measured by the percentage of educated workers, tended to have much better management practices.
- At the country level, easing up on regulation of labor market practices tended to result in a better use of incentives by management.

Research results of this type have placed even more pressure on firms to take steps to improve their management practices in order to remain competitive with peers operating from other countries throughout the world. The growing intensity of competition has made it incumbent on firms to embrace globalization as a core strategic principle given the findings of researchers such as Bloom and Van Reenen that multinationals scored higher on management practices and performance than companies that continued to restrict their activities to their own domestic market.

Management and Leadership

One threshold question that should be addressed when studying management systems and practices is the differences between "management" and "leadership" and, correspondingly, the distinctions between "managers" and "leaders" in the context of operating an organization.[17] One way to approach this topic is to review some of the opinions of various researchers and commentators who have devoted a substantial amount of time to the topic of leadership and understanding just what makes an "effective leader." For example, Bennis has said: "There is a profound difference between management and leadership, and both are important. To manage means to bring about, to accomplish, to have charge of or responsibility for, to conduct. Leading is influencing, guiding in a direction, course, action, opinion. The distinction is crucial." Bennis has also compiled the following list of differences between managers and leaders[18]:

- The manager administers; the leader innovates.
- The manager is a copy; the leader is an original.
- The manager maintains; the leader develops.
- The manager focuses on systems and structure; the leader focuses on people.

---

[17] Portions of the discussion in this section are adapted from material in Ambler, G. April 8, 2008. "Leaders vs. Managers ... Are they Really Different?" *The Practice of Leadership*, https://georgeambler.com/leaders-vs-managers-are-they-really-different/ (accessed December 31, 2018).

[18] Bennis, W. 1989. *On Becoming a Leader*. Reading, MA: Addison-Wesley.

- The manager relies on control; the leader inspires trust.
- The manager accepts reality; the leader investigates it.
- The manager has a short-range view; the leader has a long-range perspective.
- The manager asks how and when; the leader asks what and why.
- The manager has his or her eye always on the bottom line; the leader has his or her eye on the horizon.
- The manager imitates; the leader originates.
- The manager accepts the status quo; the leader challenges it.
- The manager is the classic good soldier; the leader is his or her own person.
- The manager does things right; the leader does the right thing.

Kotter has also addressed the distinction between management and leadership. After joining Bennis in noting the importance of both activities: "Leadership and management are two distinctive and complementary systems of action ... Both are necessary for success in an increasingly complex and volatile business environment." Kotter elaborates on some of the differences: "Management is about coping with complexity ... Without good management, complex enterprises tend to become chaotic ... Good management brings a degree of order and consistency ... Leadership, by contrast, is about coping with change .. More change always demands more leadership."[19] Kotter also provided a short list of some of the principal activities associated with management and leadership, noting the manager, who is concerned with managing complexity, is expected to focus on planning and budgeting, organizing and staffing, and controlling and problem-solving while the leader, who should be guiding his or her organization through "constructive change," must be adept at setting the direction for the organization (i.e., a vision of the future and strategies that should be followed to achieve that vision) and

---

[19] Kotter, J.P. 1999. on *What Leaders Really Do*. Cambridge, MA: Harvard Business Publishing.

aligning the human resources of the organization and motivating and inspiring them to move in the direction established by the leader.[20]

The topic of "leaders versus managers" was also explored by Zaleznik, whose views were described in the following way by Estill: "The difference between managers and leaders, he wrote, lies in the conceptions they hold, deep in the psyches, of chaos and order. Managers embrace process, seek stability and control, and instinctively try to resolve problems quickly— sometimes before they fully understand a problem's significance. Leaders, in contrast, tolerate chaos and lack of structure and are willing to delay closure in order to understand the issues more fully in this way, Zalenznik argued, business leaders have much more in common with artists, scientists and other creative thinkers than they do with managers. Organizations need both managers and leaders to succeed, but developing both requires a reduced focus on logic and strategic exercises in favour of an environment where creativity and imagination are permitted to flourish."[21]

History and Evolution of Management Studies

In order to understand management studies, it is useful to have some sense of the historical development of "management" (see Table 1.1). There is debate about how the "history of management" should be presented. Some argue that it is appropriate to focus primarily on the antecedents of the management tools that are widely used today, which means that management "begins" with the works of some of the classical economists in the eighteenth century and then really takes hold with the blooming of the Industrial Revolution in the nineteenth century, which ushered in the separation of ownership and management and the need to rely on professional managers using increasingly sophisticated tools for planning and controlling the activities within their organizations. Others point out

---

[20] Id.

[21] Estill, J. July 18, 2011. "Managers and Leaders—Are They Different?" *CEO Blog—Time Leadership*, http://jimestill.com/2008/03/managers-and-leaders-are-they-different.html (accessed December 31, 2018) (citing, Zaleznik, A. 1977. "Managers and Leaders: Are They Different?" *Harvard Business Review* 55, no. 3, pp. 67–78).

Table 1.1 History and Evolution of Management Studies

Pre-industrial: Evidence of sophisticated management and planning techniques used by Egyptians to create magnificent pyramids, roads, canals, and cities. Roman Empire and China also relied upon uniform formal rules, policies, and processes for security and expansive military campaigns, public works projects, and education. However, because of low value placed on commerce and business, both Greeks and Romans had little regard for trade and commerce.

Renaissance and Reformation: Rise of "mercantilism" accompanied by development of supply and production chains and accounting systems. The "Protestant Ethic" emerged, which emphasized work and engagement in continuous physical and mental labor, self-discipline, and pursuit and wise use of wealth.

Industrial Revolution: New technologies combined with changes in social, political, and legal conditions to create an economic infrastructure that relied on the power of machines rather than humans and animals. Large industrial organizations arose and technical and engineering advances caused work to become highly specialized. Firms began engaging in continuous research and development activities to solve technical problems and disseminated information and solutions to other firms, thus accelerating the rate of technological advances.

Adam Smith: Championed the then-radical notion that people should be allowed to follow their own self-interest in the commercial arena without excessive government interference in the market and highlighted the influence of organizational design and structure on productivity (i.e., division of labor and specialization).

Capitalism in America: Early Industrial Revolution activities in the United States included implementation of the "Waltham system" in Massachusetts, which featured women and child laborers and indoctrination in the moral advantages of factory work, and impressive inventive breakthroughs that included not only technologies and products necessary for establishing new industries and revolutionizing existing industries but also improvements to the transport and communications infrastructure. In order to take advantage of opportunities to expand into larger and more remote markets, American firms introduced division of labor and specialization, standardization, quality control procedures, cost accounting and work planning. The first attempt at creating and offering formalized training in "management" was launched by Wharton in 1881 and first formal master's degree program in management—the "MBA"—introduced at the Harvard Business School in 1921.

Railroads and the rise of professional management: In the United States, railroads served as the foundation for many elements of the modern business enterprise including the corporation with its hallmark feature of separation of ownership from management and the recognition of the previously nonexistent "professional manager." Management and operation of railroads required a large number of professional "middle managers" to assist in planning and coordination and oversee operational activities along portions of the track and/or markets identified by reference to particular stations along the line. In addition, the organizational structure had to account for and support a large array of specialized tasks and activities and larger railroads began to abandon the traditional functional structures in favor of multidivisional structures built on a multilevel hierarchy of managers all engaged in a range of coordination and control activities.

Table 1.1 (Continued)

Classical management theory: Classical management theory focused on finding the "one best way" to perform and manage tasks and developed in two branches referred to as "classical scientific" and "classical administrative." The classical scientific school, championed by Taylor, emphasized finding ways to increase productivity and efficiency and was based on the belief that it was possible to examine the work process and the skills of workers and develop the "best way" to get the most work done in an efficient manner. Proponents of, and contributors to, the classical administrative school (e.g., Weber, Fayol, and Follett) were more interested in developing universal management principles that could make the operation of the entire organization, rather than individual workers, more efficient and introduced new ideas about the specific functions and roles of managers, promoting participation by employees in decisions and the need for managers to focus on the development and motivation of people rather than on mechanical techniques.

Behavioral management theory: Proponents of behavioral management theories (e.g., Mayo, Barnard, Maslow, and McGregor), sometimes referred to as the "human relations movement" because of the emphasis on the human dimension of work, believed that the key to increasing productivity was to pay more attention to issues such as motivation, conflict, expectations, and group dynamics. Behavioral management theorists made a clear and substantial break from the predecessors in the classical schools by recognizing that employees are not simply machines but are individuals who should be considered resources of the organization to be nurtured, developed, and positively motivated to act in ways that would benefit the firm and satisfy their individual needs for esteem, self-fulfillment and self-actualization.

Quantitative school of management: Quantitative management theorists and researchers relied on sophisticated quantitative techniques, such as statistics information models and computer simulations, to develop methods that managers could use to improve the quality of their decision making activities. There are a number of different branches of the quantitative school including management science, operations management, management information systems (MIS), and systems management theory.

Contingency school of management: Proponents of the contingency school of management believed that there is no single best way to manage and that what constitutes the most appropriate and effective management decision or action at a given time would depend on the situational factors confronting the manager such as the type of organization, business purpose and activities of the organization, size of the organization, operating environment, corporate and societal culture, information technology and communication, and the personal style and behavior of the owner or chief executive.

Quality school of management: The quality school of management focused on "continuous improvement" of quality and performance to meet and exceed the needs and expectations of customers. Two well-known quality-based initiatives are the Kaizen (pronounced "ky-zen") and reengineering approaches. In order for quality management approaches to be successful, the organizational culture must create an environment in which all employees work together in harmony and seek to develop and maintain cooperative relationships with their peers and everyone above or below them in the organizational hierarchy.

that economic and military activities have been raising issues of planning, directing, and control for thousands of years and that one can find useful illustrations of management in the building of the pyramids in ancient Egypt, the operation of the complex trade routes during the Middle Ages, and the commercial activities of the wealthy family businesses throughout the Renaissance.

Pre-Industrial

One can find examples of managerial activities, often quite impressive and of a scope difficult to image today, going well back into pre-industrial times.[22] A number of scholars are diligently studying the history of Ancient Egypt, a society that is believed to have relied on a strong bureaucratized central state to create magnificent pyramids, roads, canals, and cities. Historians have found evidence of sophisticated management and planning techniques being used by Egyptian officials including predictions of weather events, forecasts of crops, and budgeting based on projections of tax revenues. China has contributed a legacy of a large and efficient civil service that managed a vast territory using uniform formal policies that anticipated the processes seen in modern global firms. China also produced Sun Tsu, a 13th century military strategist and historian who wrote a handbook called the *Art of War*, which is a regular part of the assigned reading for management students learning about strategy. The Roman Empire served as the foundation for management and governance of modern nations and its state hierarchy introduced rules and processes that were adroitly used for security and expansive military campaigns, public works projects, and education. The reign of the Medici family in Italy featured its own unique set of somewhat brutal managerial practices, which were described near the turn of the 16th century by Machiavelli in *The Prince*, a book that is also still widely read by management students.

---

[22] Elements of the discussion of the history of pre-industrial management are derived from essays prepared by E. Makamson on the topic and included in Makamson, E. 2000. *The History of Management: The Rise of the Professional Manager in America*.

While the achievements of rulers, generals, and senior government ministers during pre-industrial times are impressive, particularly given the challenges confronting them with respect to resources, there is little from that period that qualifies as "business management." Historians have attributed this to the low value that was placed on commerce and business noting, for example, that both the Greeks and the Romans have little regard for trade and commerce. For example, the Greeks denied citizenship to manual workers and merchants and their activities were generally performed by foreigners and slaves. While the Romans did promote the formation of joint stock companies, they were used only to raise capital for projects undertaken by the state and could not be established for private enterprise. The early Church made it difficult to borrow money for mercantile activities by prohibiting usury (i.e., charging interest on borrowed money). With prospective entrepreneurs deprived of opportunities to attract capital to support any private business ventures, most areas relied heavily on agricultural production rather than manufactured goods, and aristocrats and bureaucrats were allowed to govern in traditional ways without much need for business management principles.

Renaissance and Reformation: Rise of Mercantilism

The disdain for commercial activities and preoccupation with local markets continued during most of the Middle Ages; however, important changes arose out of the Crusades that brought feudal Europe in contact with the East and exposed Europeans to trading opportunities that formed the foundation for "mercantilism." Mercantilism had existed in a primitive form within the Roman Empire but beginning in the later part of the 13th century Europeans proactively established and expanded trade systems across North Africa, Spain, the Middle East, and Asia. In fact, the focus of warfare shifted from political and religious objectives to seizing and controlling trade routes. Once the Renaissance began, merchants began to develop the first supply and production chains using raw materials obtained from the East, which were sent to individual workers or families who used their own equipment to produce finished goods that were delivered to the merchants in exchange for wages. This domestic production system spawned the first accounting systems and the first book on "double entry bookkeeping" appeared in 1494 from the hand of a Venetian mathematician named Luca Paciolo. Restrictions on lending began to erode and large banks, such as those operated by the Peruzzi and Medici families in Italy, provided funding for businesses and a safe and efficient means for transferring funds between accounts to complete commercial transactions.[23]

While mercantilism was a dramatic and welcome development, it remained a tool that largely benefitted the state and not individual merchants or workers. According to Colbert, writing in the late 17th century, the characteristics of mercantilism included "bullionism," favorable balance of trade, economic self-sufficiency, agriculture as the basis for national wealth, tariffs, national power emanating from a strong navy and colonies that provided captive markets for manufactured goods, and sources of raw material and recognition of the state as the guide for economic development through the promulgation and enforcement of economic and trade policies.[24] To the extent that large-scale enterprises existed, they operated in the form of state monopolies as part of the government's economic development role. However, the joint stock companies formed to pursue financial opportunities, particularly in the colonies, eventually became the model for capitalizing private corporations. In addition, the Reformation undermined the prescriptions of the Roman Church and encouraged uprising against traditional authorities that eventually led to a new social order that recognized the value of the individual. Max Weber later wrote about the "Protestant Ethic" and the impact that it had on the emergence of what came to be known as "capitalism" in his 1905 book titled *The Protestant Ethic and the Spirit of Capitalism* and noted that Protestants were taught to emphasize work and engage

---

[23] Elements of the discussion of the rise of mercantilism during the Renaissance and Reformation are derived from essays prepared by E. Makamson on the topic and included in Makamson, E. 2000. *The History of Management: The Rise of the Professional Manager in America.*

[24] Mercantilism is so closely associated with Colbert, the chief minister of French king Louis XIV for over 20 years during the late 17th century, that it is also often referred to as "Colbertism." See Ames, G.J. 1996. *Colbert, Mercantilism and the French Quest for the Asian Trade.* DeKalb, IL: Northern Illinois University Press.

in continuous physical and mental labor, take responsibility for finding and pursuing their "calling," practice self-discipline, and pursue and use wealth wisely in order to obtain salvation.

Industrial Revolution

A number of the basic elements of modern management began to take root during the Industrial Revolution, which is generally thought to have taken place during the period beginning around 1750 and ending in 1870.[25] New technologies combined with changes in social, political, and legal conditions to create an economic infrastructure that relied on the power of machines rather than humans and animals. Large industrial organizations arose and work became highly specialized. In Great Britain, often thought to be the birthplace of the Industrial Revolution, laws were implemented to recognize and protect private and intellectual property, taxes were reduced to relatively modest levels in relation to other parts of Europe, the powers of the King were limited, and government policies toward matters of commerce were relatively "hands off." The Bank of England, which was the central bank, actively promoted economic development through the issuance of currency and the creation of stable national monetary system. In general, citizens were given more freedom to engage in entrepreneurial risk-taking and pursue the creation of wealth through commercial activities.

An important development during the 18th century was the evolution of the joint stock company, previously used only for state-controlled activities, into what eventually became the modern corporation. The drive to harvest the vast natural resources believed to exist in the colonies created an urgent need for capital, which was satisfied by the sale of stocks in private companies. Orderly exchange of these stocks was facilitated by the expansion of exchanges throughout Europe beyond commodities and currencies to include stocks in commercial ventures. During the mid-19th century, new laws were passed to limit the liability of investors and require

---

[25] Elements of the discussion of management during the Industrial Revolution are derived from essays prepared by E. Makamson on the topic and included in Makamson, E. 2000. *The History of Management: The Rise of the Professional Manager in America.*

that managers of companies provide a public accounting of profits and losses and how funds raised through stock offerings were actually invested.

However, the defining events of the Industrial Revolution were the technical and engineering achievements that transformed the way that work was done throughout Europe and, eventually, the entire world. In 1765, James Watt improved on the prior work of others to develop the first workable steam engine that provided a reliable source of power for use in a wide range of industrial activities. Perhaps just as important was Watt's partnership with Boulton, which not only focused on manufacturing of steam engines but also on continuous research and development activities to solve technical problems and, quite significantly, disseminate information and solutions to other firms. The sharing of information and widespread collaboration, a familiar sight today, was a radical change in the way commercial activities were carried out and accelerated the rate of the technological advances. The introduction of the steam engine freed manufacturers from the need to be close to sources of water power and allowed them to set up operations almost anywhere. Improvements in rail and steamship services supported transport of raw materials and finished goods. The Industrial Revolution even sowed the seeds of the later computer revolution with the invention of the first mechanical calculator, predecessor to the modern computer, by Babbage in 1822.

Adam Smith

The economic theory underlying much of what occurred during the Industrial Revolution was provided in the work of so-called classical economists such as Adam Smith, whose seminar work—*An Inquiry into the Nature and Causes of the Wealth of Nations*—was published in 1776 as the Industrial Revolution was just taking off. Simply put, Smith believed that people wanted to follow their own self-interest and that they should be allowed to do so in the commercial arena without excessive interference from the government (i.e., the government should take a "liassez faire attitude" toward the market). The essential terms of what eventually became known as Smith's version of "capitalism" include the following[26]:

---

[26] E. Makamson, "Adam Smith" in Makamson, E. 2000. *The History of Management: The Rise of the Professional Manager in America.*

1. Private ownership and control of the means of production, including land and the plant and equipment used to produce goods and services (plant and equipment were referred to in Smith's work as "capital").
2. "Markets" are the foundation for organization and coordination of the economy and consist of direct interactions between buyers and sellers (producers).
3. Suppliers, which include both the owners of land and capital and laborers offering and providing their services, pursue their own self-interest with the goal of maximizing their gain and profits from the use of their resources.
4. Buyers of the goods and services offered by suppliers also pursue their self-interest and seek to spend their money in ways that maximize their satisfaction.
5. Suppliers and buyers reconcile their simultaneous pursuit of their self-interest by "haggling" over the value of the goods and services in order to establish the price at which exchanges can occur.

Smith believed that a competitive market that includes buyers and sellers both pursuing their own self-interest would be self-regulating and that there was little need for government to intervene in the marketplace. Smith suggested that the state should focus its efforts on "public goods" and other activities that would protect society and its private markets, including a military force to protect from foreign attack, a police force to protect private property rights, laws to guarantee contracts, and, when necessary, support for "infrastructure" projects that benefit everyone (i.e., roads and canals). Smith's ideas were clearly at odds with the mercantilism that dominated most parts of Europe during the early years of the Industrial Revolution. Moreover, Smith's theories assumed that individuals were linked together and organized into communities through economic markets, a far different formulation from the views of philosophers such as Locke and Rousseau who envisioned a "social contract" in which the state played a powerful role in creating and unifying communities of individuals.

Smith also took note of concepts that have become the lynchpins of discussions regarding organizational design and structure. He specifically emphasized the progress that had been made with respect to productivity and attributed it to the discovery and development of new manufacturing technologies and innovations that had occurred in the way that work activities were organized. Specifically, he focused on how the division of labor that occurred on the assembly line permitted necessary tasks and activities to be done more quickly due to specialization as well as the way that machinery reduced the time and number of works required to complete activities. One thing that Smith did not build into his model was the concept of "management" as a valuable and distinguishable activity and he, like many others, assumed that the owner and manager were one and the same.[27]

Capitalism in America

The initial activities of the European nations with their colonies in America focused on a variety of trade opportunities primarily for the benefit of the home country.[28] Spain concentrated on the areas of West of the Mississippi and South America; the Dutch and Swedes were interested in fur trading along the Hudson River and in Delaware, respectively; and the English set up the London and Plymouth companies to develop Virginia and England, respectively. The early efforts of the English colonies failed to achieve the expected and desired financial success and eventually investors in England either gave up or allowed their stakes to be repurchased by the colonists, which left the economic future of colonies largely in the hands of the settlers who had been granted stock and land. Entrepreneurism took hold quickly and the colonies were soon engaged in a wide range of trading activities, which have been described as follows: "The early colonial enterprise rested largely on the triangular trade routes:

---

[27] Other economists followed Smith during the nineteenth century to make additional contributions to the theoretical underpinnings of economics and management. For example, Mill wrote about resource allocation, production and pricing issues and other well-known scholars of the time included Marshall and Walras.

[28] Elements of the discussion of capitalism in America are derived from essays prepared by E. Makamson on the topic and included in Makamson, E. 2000. *The History of Management: The Rise of the Professional Manager in America.*

rum to Africa from New York and Philadelphia, people from Africa to Cuba, and molasses and coin from Cuba to New York/Philadelphia; and, sugar and molasses to England from Cuba, manufactured goods from England to New York/Philadelphia, and grains and meat from New York/ Philadelphia to Cuba."[29] However, England repeatedly interfered with the economic interests of its colonies through mercantilist policies, particularly taxes on exports and imports, eventually leading to the rebellion that culminated in the independence of the colonies and the creation of the United States.

The Constitution of the United States provided an opportunity for the founders to develop a blueprint for economic activities in the new nation. The Constitution provided for a limited national government; however, it still had the power and authority to regulate interstate commerce, control national defense, and impose taxes. Individual economic rights could be found throughout the Constitution, including private intellectual property rights (i.e., patents and copyrights), restrictions on the ability of the national government to seize property without "due process," and prohibitions on attempts by the states to interfere with contractual obligations. There was real debate, however, about the preferred direction for national business development and the role that the central government would play in that development. Jefferson, who came out of the Southern plantation society, had a preference for continuing to focus on agricultural activities and wrote about his preference to "let our workshops remain in Europe." In contrast, Hamilton from the North argued for a strong national government and a national bank that would serve as the focal point for an economic policy that relied on mustering available land, labor, and foreign capital to pursue industrialization. While Hamilton's national bank for economic development was never created, the United States eventually entered the Industrial Revolution on the back of a burgeoning textiles industry built on technology first brought from England by Slater, improved by Whitney and his cotton gin and innovatively implemented by the "Waltham system" in Massachusetts, which featured women and child laborers and indoctrination in the moral advantages of factory work.

---

[29] Id.

America's industrial prowess soon grew beyond textiles through the amazing and wide-ranging activities of its own inventors throughout the nineteenth century. American inventors not only devised the technologies and products necessary for establishing new industries and revolutionizing existing industries, they also facilitated improvements to the transport and communications infrastructure required for trading volumes to accelerate and for information, raw materials, people, and finished goods to move efficiently around the country. Well-known examples include the steamboat (Fitch (1789) and Fulton (1807)); iron plow (Wood (1817)); reaper (McCormick (1831)); electric motor (Davenport (1834)); telegraph (Morse (1844)); sewing machine (Howe (1849)); Pullman car (Pullman (1858)); suspension bridge (Roebling (1868)); refrigerated freight car (Swift (1875)); telephone (Bell (1876)); gasoline carriage, the precursor to the automobile (Selden (1879)); the Kodak camera (Kodak (1880)); and the light bulb (Edison (1880)).[30]

Historians have referred to the period during which these inventions appeared as the Second Industrial Revolution, a time when steam technologies gave way to advances in other areas of manufacturing and the emergence of the power of electricity. The numbers support this categorization by showing that the number of industrial wage earners in the United States grew from 957,000 in 1849 to 4,252,000 in 1889 and that by 1894 the United States was the world leader in the value of factory-made goods. Industrialization also had a dramatic impact on the demographic profile of the United States: in 1840 8.5% of the population lived in 44 cities; however, by 1890 urbanization had increased dramatically as 32% of the population was then living in 547 cities.[31]

Technological innovation was accompanied by improvements in production processes that were needed to support the pace of manufacturing and attempts by American firms to expand into larger and more remote markets. For example, this period saw the introduction of standardization, quality control procedures, cost accounting, work planning, and "interchangeable parts." The factory system first developed in the textile industry quickly spread to all market-oriented industries in the United

---

[30] Id.

[31] Id.

States by the 1860s and 1870s[32] and featured mass manufacturing by power-driven machines in a way that became known as the "American system of manufacturing."[33] The lack of uniformity on the factory floor that had been the hallmark of activities at the beginning of the century had disappeared in favor increasingly sophisticated methods for effectively applying the powerful concepts of division of labor, specialization, and mechanization. Another interesting development was the first attempt at creating and offering formalized training in "management" launched by Wharton in 1881 when he underwrote a new business school at the University of Pennsylvania; however, the "Wharton school" did not have professors and the only literature it offered was "how to" manuals and trade publications and it was not until 1921 that the first formal master's degree program in management—the "MBA"—would be introduced at the Harvard Business School.

Railroads and the Rise of Professional Management

The ongoing industrial transformation that was occurring in the United States was accompanied by similar progress in England and Germany and in each instance the development of the railroad industry played a major role. What was different about the United States, however, was the way in which its railroads served as the foundation for many elements of the modern business enterprise, particularly the corporation. The size of the railroads in the United States, and the amount of capital invested for expansion and improvements, was extremely impressive and by the late 1880s the Pennsylvania RR, for example, employed over 50,000 workers and railroads in general had been operated profitably for decades. Also of interest in the context of the discussion of organizational structure and governance was the reliance that railroads placed on incorporating so that they could sell stock to investors to raise the substantial amount of capital

[32] Nelson, D. 1980. *Taylor and Scientific Management*. Madison, WI: The University of Wisconsin Press.

[33] Woodbury, R. 1972. "The Legend of Eli Whitney and Interchangeable Parts." In *Technology and Culture*, M. Kranzberg and W. Davenport, 318–36. New York, NY: Schocken Books.

that their businesses managers required. By the middle of nineteenth century more than half of the negotiable securities in the United States had been offered and sold by railroads and transactions in rail stocks were key factors in the establishment of the main US financial markets on Wall Street and in Philadelphia. These developments were important because they legitimized the hallmark feature of the corporate form—separation of ownership from management—and ushered in the era of the previously nonexistent "professional manager."[34]

The size and complexity of the US market and the corresponding need for rail lines that extended for thousands of miles impacted not only the amount of capital that was required but also the way that railroads were managed and operated. The need for comprehensive planning and coordination to complete projects such as the "transcontinental railroad" undertaken by the Union Pacific and Central Pacific called for large number of professional "middle managers" who were charged with overseeing operational activities along portions of the track and/or markets identified by reference to particular stations along the line. In addition, the organizational structure had to account for and support all of the specialized tasks and activities that needed to be completed in order for the railroad to perform efficiently such as scheduling, pricing, the logistics of handling passengers and freight, maintenance, and establishment and enforcement of corporate policies. All of this called for attention to division and specialization of labor that has become a dominant feature of modern organizational design.

McCallum, who managed the Erie line for the New York and Erie Railroad Company, analyzed the progress and requirements of organizational structure for railroad and proposed what became the first principles for organization of the "modern" corporation in the mid-1850s in his reports to the board of directors. He did this by comparing and contrasting the "functional" organizational structure, which theretofore had been the dominant form used by many enterprises, with the emerging

---

[34] Elements of the discussion of the rise of professional management in America are derived from essays prepared by E. Makamson on the topic and included in Makamson, E. 2000. *The History of Management: The Rise of the Professional Manager in America.*

"multidivisional" organizational structure that was being developed to address the specific needs of the larger railroads. The functional structure, which allocates and organizes labor and other resources based on function or task, was thought to be suitable only for smaller businesses operating in a single market and selling a single product.

McCallum argued that the functional structure might be suitable for rail lines that were relatively short, say no longer than 500 miles, because it was still possible for one superintendent to effectively oversee operations[35]; however, when a railroad reached the point where it was operating on a much larger scale the preferred organizational approach was adoption of a multidivisional structure. When applied to railroads, the multidivisional structure operated as follows:

- Rail lines were broken up into manageable pieces, which were placed into geographical divisions that were managed by a divisional supervisor, thereby allowing each division to be efficiently operated in much the same way as a small business.
- Each divisional supervisor reported to headquarters, which ensured that information from each division was being collected and analyzed for facilitate planning and coordination for the entire railroad.
- The planning and coordination activities occurring at head-quarters were facilitated by development of "staff" functions concentrating on planning, financial controls, and develop-ment and implementation of general business policies.

The multidivision structure, with multiple operating units in different locations carrying out different activities and reporting to a centralized

---

[35] He explain that: "[a] superintendent of a road 50 miles in length can give its business his professional attention and may be constantly on the line engaged in die direction of its details; each person is personally known to him, and all questions in relation to its business are at once presented and acted upon; and any system however imperfect may under such circumstances prove comparatively successful." As quoted in Chandler, A. 1962. *Strategy and Structure: Chapters in the History of the American Industrial Enterprise*. Cambridge, MA: MIT Press.

headquarters unit eventually became the preferred model for US companies operating in other industries that grew and expanded into new markets and product lines. This development confirmed and solidified the role of "professional manager" since the multidivisional structure was built on a multilevel hierarchy of managers—senior managers at the top, middle managers at each level and line managers interacting directly with workers—who all engaged in a range of coordination and control activities with respect to the piece of the operations for which they were responsible with the common goal of achieving the goals and objectives of the entire firm.

Classical Management Theory

The Industrial Revolution and the rise of the "factory system" created a number of challenges and problems for managers, notably questions about how to organize and oversee the myriad range of tasks that needed to be performed by a continuously expanding group of workers. Managers needed ways to cope with training and motivating workers, a problem that was made all the more difficult in the United States as more and more non-English-speaking immigrants entered the workforce, and diffuse worker dissatisfaction with factory conditions and their role in designing their jobs. The first attempts to solve these issues came from what has come to be referred to as "classical management theory," which focused on finding the "one best way" to perform and manage tasks and developed in two branches referred to as "classical scientific" and "classical administrative."

Taylor and "Scientific Management"

The "classical scientific" school is known for its emphasis on finding ways to increase productivity and efficiency and its belief that it was possible to examine the work process and the skills of workers and develop the "best way" to get the most work done in an efficient manner. The most well-known contributor to this school is Frederick Winslow Taylor (1856–1915), who has often been referred to as the "Father of Modern Management" and widely recognized as one of the first management theorists.[36] His background was in engineering and he had spent time as a common laborer and apprentice foreman before rising to the level of chief engineer. As such, it was not surprising that his theories were based on the fundamental premise that that human labor could be organized and managed in much the same way as machine work and that the activities of workers can and should be "engineered" in order to achieve efficiency and productivity. Taylor argued that "inefficiency" caused losses not only for firms but the country as a whole and provided the following explanation for why he wrote the essays that appeared in his *Principles of Scientific Management*, which was published in 1911[37]:

> First: To point out, through a series of simple illustrations, the great loss which the whole country is suffering through inefficiency in almost all of our daily acts. Second: To try to convince the reader that the remedy for this inefficiency lies in systematic management, rather than in searching for some unusual or extraordinary man. Third: To prove that the best management is a true science, resting upon clearly defined laws, rules, and principles, as a foundation... . The illustrations chosen are such as, it is believed, will especially appeal to engineers and to managers of industrial and manufacturing establishments, and also quite as much to all of the men who are working in these establishments. It is hoped, however, that it will be clear to other readers that the same principles can be applied with equal force to all social activities: to the management of our homes; the management of our farms; the management of the business of our tradesmen, large and small; of our churches, our philanthropic institutions, our universities, and our governmental departments.

---

[36] Elements of the discussion of Taylor and "Scientific Management" are derived from essays prepared by E. Makamson on the topic and included in Makamson, E. 2000. *The History of Management: The Rise of the Professional Manager in America.*

[37] Taylor, F.W. 1911. *The Principles of Scientific Management*, 5–29. New York, NY: Harper Bros.

In his book *Shop Management*, which was published in 1903, Taylor began with the argument that workers were inefficient for several reasons. First, he believed that workers tended to ration their work load or work less than they should because if they worked harder and faster there would be no work to do in the future and they would not have any source of income in the future. Second, he blamed management for failing to structure work activities effectively and not providing appropriate incentives for workers.[38] It should be noted that at that time firms tended to compensate workers using a daily or hourly rate, a practice that Taylor felt rewarded workers for simply showing up and not for their actual performance from a production perspective. "Piece-rate" compensation was also used in some instances; however, this approach was often not effective due to the failure to set and maintain adequate quality standards.[39]

Taylor believed that worker inefficiency could be solved by observing how the work is performed to determine the appropriate work standard and then fitting the compensation for the work to the standard. This required a careful investigation of each job by dividing it into discrete tasks in order to identify the most efficient way to perform that task and then reconstructing all of the tasks into an efficient job. Taylor used time and motion studies and advised that once the best method for performing a job had been identified, it should be recorded so that procedures could

---

[38] Taylor explained that workers failed to act "efficiently" when performing their jobs for several reasons: "First: The fallacy, which has from time immemorial been almost universal among workmen, that a material increase in the output of each man or each machine in the trade would result in the end in throwing a large number of men out of work. Second: The defective systems of management which are in common use, and which make it necessary for each workman to soldier, or work slowly, in order that he may protect his own best interests. Third: The inefficient rule-of-thumb methods, which are still almost universal in all trades and in practicing which our workmen waste a large part of their effort." Taylor, F.W. 1911. *The Principles of Scientific Management*, 5–29. New York, NY: Harper Bros.

[39] Makamson explained that the "piece-rate" system "generally failed because standards were poorly set, employers cut rates when workers earned 'too much', and workers would conceal their real capacity for production to keep standards low."

be taught to all of the workers who would be asked to perform the same activity. Managers could do their part by setting specific performance targets for their workers, paying them for meeting those targets and providing workers with regular feedback on their performance. The main elements of Taylor's theory have been explained as follows[40]:

1. Management is a true science. The solution to the problem of determining fair work standards and practices could be discovered by experimentation and observation. From this, it follows, that there is "one right way" for work to be performed.
2. The selection of workers is a science. Taylor's "first class worker" was someone suitable for the job. It was management's role to determine the kind of work for which an employee was most suited, and to hire and assign workers accordingly.
3. Workers are to be developed and trained. It is management's task to not only engineer a job that can be performed efficiently, but management is responsible for training the worker as to how the work is to be performed and for updating practices as better ones are developed. This standardizes how the work is performed in the best way.
4. Scientific management is a collaboration of workers and managers. Managers are not responsible for execution of work, but they are responsible for how the work is done. Planning, scheduling, methods, and training are functions of the manager.

Taylor wrote that the process of job design provided an opportunity for collaboration between labor and management, which would generate more wealth for everyone involved; however, critics claimed that workers had little or no input into selecting their jobs, or how their jobs were designed, and that this ultimately led to higher levels of worker alienation. Labor unions saw "Taylorism" as exploitive and his approach eventually fell out of favor in the United States as unions pushed for minimum hourly wage guarantees that were at odds with the "pay for performance" approach, which was implicit in Taylor's system. Nonetheless,

---

[40] Makamson, E. 2000. "Taylor and Scientific Management." In *The History of Management: The Rise of the Professional Manager in America.*

it is generally conceded that Taylor made a major contribution to elevating management to a level that it was considered a legitimate subject for scholarly work and professional practice. Moreover, while scientific management ran into significant opposition in the United States and Europe, Taylor's theories were quite influential in other parts of the world. For example, Taylor was quite popular in Japan where Yoichi Ueno introduced Taylorism in 1912 and went on to create what became known as the "Japanese management style." Ueno's son Ichiro later pioneered quality assurance in Japan.

While Taylor is the most celebrated and discussed proponent of the classical scientific school, others also made significant, interesting, and sometimes controversial contributions. Gantt, an associate of Taylor, developed the "Gantt chart," which is still in use today as a tool for graphing the scheduling of tasks and work flows and thus providing managers with a means for carrying out their planning and controlling roles. The Gilbreths, a husband-and-wife team, developed photographic methods for conducting "time and motion" studies that could be used to break down and analyze each component action associated with a particular task in order to identify the "best way" to perform specific tasks and entire jobs. The results of these studies were used to reorganize each component action so that the entire tasks could be performed more efficiently and with less time and effort.[41] The Gilbreths were also pioneers in the study of fatigue in the workplace and led the way in analyzing how the physical characteristics of the environment in which employees worked (i.e., lighting, heating, color of walls, and design of tools and machines) might contribute to their job stress.[42] Other contributors included Munsterberg, the founder of the discipline of industrial psychology, and McKinsey, the

---

[41] Jones, G., and J. George. 2017. *Essentials of Contemporary Management*, 10th ed. New York, NY: McGraw-Hill Professional Publishing. Appendix A ("History of Management Thought") to Chapter 1.

[42] See Gilbreth, F., and L. Gilbreth. 1919. *Fatigue Study: The Elimination of Humanity's Greatest Waste—A First Step in Motion Study*. New York, NY: The Macmillan Company. For a contemporary survey of research on the effects of the physical environment on job performance, see Vischer, J. 2007. "The Effects of the Physical Environment on Job Performance: Towards a Theoretical Model of Workspace Stress." *Stress and Health* 23, no. 3, p. 175.

developer of budgeting practices used as a means of accountability and measurement of performance.

Classical Administrative School

While the focus of scientific management was on increasing the efficiency of production and the productivity of individual workers, proponents of the classical administrative school were more interested in developing universal management and organizational design principles that could make the operation of the entire organization more efficient and effective. One of the earliest, and well-known, contributors to the administrative school was Max Weber. Weber wrote extensively about his ideas regarding the definition and benefits of bureaucratic administration of organizations.[43] Weber was one of the first to argue that businesses should not allow their managers to exercise control arbitrarily and without any explanation to the impacted workers. He believed that rational legal authority was the preferred approach to control within an organization and that "bureaucracy" was the most efficient form of organization. While bureaucracy today has a negative connotation and is generally associated with organizational practices that are slow and inflexible, Weber championed bureaucracy to his contemporaries as a necessary and preferred alternative to the other forms of authority, which he believed led to unfairness within the workplace and corruption among those in authority at major corporations during the late nineteenth century.

Another important figure in the classical administrative school was Henri Fayol, who promulgated a detailed set of "principles of management" as another means for effectively controlling an organization. His ideas touched on many of the topics that are still hotly debated in the world of organizational design and did so in a way that recognized that there are trade-offs that must be made when creating the optimal structure for an

---

[43] Weber, M. 1946. "Bureaucracy." In *From Max Weber*, eds. Hans Gerth and C. Wright Mills, 196–244. New York, NY: Oxford University Press. See also Weber, M. 1947. *The Theory of Social and Economic Organization, Translated by A. M. Henderson & Talcott Parsons.* The Free Press.

organization at any point in time. Fayol was one of the first to focus on the specific functions and roles of managers and famously observed that managers had five principal roles: planning, organizing, commanding, coordinating, and controlling. He went to develop and explain fourteen "principles of administration" to be followed by managers when performing their roles including now well-known concepts such as specialization/division of labor, authority with responsibility, unity of command, unity of direction, centralization, and line of authority.[44]

Also associated with the classical administrative school is Mary Parker Follett, who was one of the first management theorists who advocated greater participation by employees in decision making and establishment of the overall goals and objectives of the organization. She disfavored the command-style hierarchical organizations advocated by her contemporaries and argued that managers should focus on the development and motivation of "people" rather than on mechanical techniques. She also argued that managers should not impose their own will on subordinates but instead should take steps to organize the groups that they oversee in a manner that allows for discovering and harmonizing the views of the members of the group. In her own words:

> The leader guides the group and is at the same time himself guided by the group, is always a part of the group. No one can truly lead except from within. ... [A leader] must be able to lead us to wise decisions, not to impose his own wise decisions upon us. We need leaders, not masters or drivers."[45] Her teachings were not widely accepted during her career; however, as time has gone by her guidelines, which ironically were not originally intended for business managers, have become part of the mainstream of contemporary management recommendations and are now widely followed by today's managers. In fact, a collection of her writings published in 2003 bears the descriptive title of "Prophet of

---

[44] Fayol, H., and C. Storrs. 1949. *General and Industrial Management*, Pitman.
[45] Follett, M. 1918. *The New State—Group Organization, the Solution for Popular Government*. University Park, PA: Pennsylvania State University Press.

Management."[46] Follett's emphasis on human relations and how managers interacted with their workers could also be easily placed within the behavioral management theories discussed in the following and she was also among the first to give serious attention to conflict resolution in the workplace.

Finally, Chester Barnard, who was president of the New Jersey Bell Telephone Company, introduced the "acceptance" theory of management, which was based on establishing conditions within the organization that led to employees accepting the legitimate authority of their managers to make decisions and set directions for the organization. Barnard argued that acceptance was based on several factors, including the ability of the employees to understand communications from their managers; employee acceptance of the communication as being consistent with the goals and purposes of the organization; the belief by employees that their actions will be consistent with the needs and desires of other employees; and the belief of employees that they are mentally and physically able to carry out orders issued by their managers. In order to achieve acceptance, managers needed to focus on developing a sense of common purpose among employees and an organizational culture that recognized the need for cooperation and valued those who were willing to cooperate to achieve the goals and purposes of the organization. Barnard also was among the first to acknowledge the existence of an "informal organization," which refers to the cliques or other groups that inevitably form within an organization and which can provide a valuable service in collecting and disseminating information. Barnard's focus on the mindset of employees was the precursor for the emergence of the next major school of management thought discussed next: behavioral management theory.[47]

---

[46] Graham, P., ed. 2003. *Mary Parker Follett Prophet of Management*. See also Mele, D. 2018. "Ethics in Management: Exploring the Contribution of Mary Parker Follett." http://iese.edu/research/pdfs/DI-0618-E.pdf (accessed December 31, 2018).

[47] See generally Barnard, C. 1938. *The Functions of the Executive*. Cambridge, MA: Harvard University Press. See also Mahoney, J. 2002. "The Relevance of Chester I. Barnard's Teachings to Contemporary Management Education: Communicating the Aesthetics of Management." *International Journal of Organizational Theory and Behavior* 5, nos. 1–2, pp. 159–72.

Behavioral Management Theory

Behavioral management theory was a response to some of the shortcomings associated with the classical theories, particularly their inability to explain the behaviors of individual employees in many situations and the lack of guidance they provided to managers with respect to motivating employees to accept and carry out their directives. Proponents of behavioral management theories, sometimes referred to as the "human relations movement" because of the emphasis on the human dimension of work, believed that the key to increasing productivity was to pay more attention to issues such as motivation, conflict, expectations, and group dynamics. In short, behavioral management theorists made a clear and substantial break from the predecessors in the classical schools by recognizing that employees are not simply machines but are individuals who should be considered resources of the organization that should be nurtured and developed. As a practical matter, this shift would mean that managers could no longer limit their activities to explaining and controlling technical aspects of the work performed by their subordinates but must instead be able to understand human needs and behavior in their organizations and the workings of the "informal organization," which is the system of behavioral rules and norms that emerge in a group and must be taken into account in any attempt to manage or change the behavior of members of the group.[48]

The foundation for behavioral management theory included studies by Mayo and others that provided evidence that human relations and the social needs of workers are important factors for effective organizational management. Mayo's studies are referred to as the "Hawthorne Studies" and were conducted from 1924 to 1932 at the Hawthorne Works of the

---

[48] Jones, G., and J. George. 2014. *Essentials of Contemporary Management,* 10th ed. New York, NY: McGraw-Hill Professional Publishing, Appendix A ("History of Management Thought") to Chapter 1. Jones and George commented that the study of informal organizations and other factors that impacted how individuals and groups responded to and acted in organizations became the focus of a research field which eventually became known as "organizational behavior."

Western Electric Company.[49] While conducting various tests to determine how characteristics of the work setting, such as lighting, influenced fatigue and performance among employees, the researchers found that their presence affected the results and that employees enjoyed the attention and were eager to cooperate with the researchers by producing the results that the employees believed the researchers were expecting. This result, which became known as the "Hawthorne effect," supported the argument that workers' performance could be positively influenced by managerial attitudes and provided a foundation for the human relations movement that was based on the proposition that managers should be trained in behaviors that elicit cooperation from employees and increased their productivity.[50] Maslow developed his well-known theory of human needs based on the assumptions that human behavior is purposeful and motivated by the need for satisfaction and that human needs could be classified according to a hierarchical structure of importance that had five levels that ranged from lowest to highest.[51] Managers with this information and understanding of the needs of their subordinates could presumably tailor their instructions in ways that were most likely to resonate with subordinates at that time and motivate them to act in the manner deemed necessary for organizational efficiency.

One of the most well-known behavioral management models is McGregor's Theory X and Theory Y, which was heavily influenced by the work of both Mayo and Maslow.[52] McGregor posited various principles that he believed managers should follow in order to increase their effectiveness in motivating employees to act in ways that would benefit the firm. He began by arguing that all managers held one of two very different views regarding the abilities and motivations of their subordinates,

---

[49] Mayo, E. 1933. *The Human Problems of an Industrial Civilization*. New York, NY: Macmillan.

[50] Jones, G., and J. George. 2017. *Essentials of Contemporary Management*, 10th ed. New York, NY: McGraw-Hill Professional Publishing. Appendix A ("History of Management Thought") to Chapter 1.

[51] See Maslow, A. 1954. *Motivation and Personality*. New York, NY: Harper.

[52] The ideas underlying Theory X and Theory Y first appeared in McGregor, D. 1960. *The Human Side of Enterprise*. New York, NY: McGraw Hill.

which he dubbed Theory X and Theory Y, and that these views influenced the way that managers treated their subordinates and the way in which subordinates performed. The key assumptions for Theory X were that the average worker: dislikes work and attempts to avoid it (i.e., "lazy"); has no ambition or desire for responsibility and prefers to follow rather than lead; is self-centered and has no interest in the goals and objectives of the firm as a whole; is untrustworthy; is resistant to change; and is gullible and lacks intelligence. The bottom line is that Theory X implicitly assumes that employees only work for money and security and that motivational policies of firms, if they can really be called that, should be confined to providing cash compensation and basic benefits and that such employees should be given little in the way of discretion and flexibility. Theory X managers closely supervise their subordinates to make sure that they work hard, create strict work rules, and implement a well-defined system of rewards and punishments in order to exert control over those who work for them.[53]

Theory Y, on the other hand, is based on the belief that employees have the higher level needs identified in Maslow's hierarchy (i.e., esteem and self-actualization) and calls for the following very different assumptions about workers and workplace: work can be as natural as play and rest; employees will be self-directed to fulfill the workplace objectives if they are personally committed to them and the requisite level of commitment can be achieved by providing rewards that address higher needs such as self-fulfillment; if employees are personally committed and properly rewarded, they will act in a responsible fashion; and workers are trustworthy and it is therefore justifiable to expect that most employees can handle responsibility since they are inherently creative and ingenuous. Firms and managers that believe in Theory Y will not only offer materialistic rewards but will also provide other opportunities for subordinates to pursue and achieve their inner needs (i.e., the needs at the top of Maslow's needs hierarchy such as social needs, ego-based needs

---

[53] Jones, G., and J. George. 2017. *Essentials of Contemporary Management*, 10th ed. New York, NY: McGraw-Hill Professional Publishing. (noting also that Henry Ford's practice of closely supervising and managing his workforce was a good illustration of Theory X management style).

and self-fulfillment). For example, such firms and managers are likely to implement strategies such as decentralization and delegation, job enlargement, participative management, and performance appraisals against objectives that are established jointly by the firm and its employees. Gareth and George explained that in Theory Y organizations "individuals and groups are still accountable for their activities, but the manager's role is not to control employees but to provide support and advice, to make sure employees have the resources they need to perform their jobs and to evaluate them on their ability to help the organization meet its goals."[54]

Quantitative School of Management

Another well-known school of management, which had its origins in research conducted during World War II by mathematicians, physicists, and other scientists, focused on finding solutions for military problems, is the "quantitative" school. Quantitative management theorists and researchers rely on sophisticated quantitative techniques, such as statistics information models, computer simulations, linear and nonlinear programming, queuing theory, and chaos theory, to develop methods that managers can use to improve the quality of their decision-making activities. For example, quantitative management tools have become essential for managers trying to determine how much inventory should be held at a particular time of the year, where to build a new factory, or how to invest the firm's capital.[55]

There are a number of different branches of the quantitative school and some of the commonly recognized include management science, which uses techniques such as mathematical forecasting for improving the planning process, inventory modeling, and queuing theory; operations management (or operations research), which focuses on the analysis of the essential process of transforming various inputs (i.e., materials,

---

[54] Id. (noting also that Fayol's approach to administration, the "principles of management" discussed earlier, reflected many of the assumptions associated with Theory Y).

[55] Jones, G., and J. George. 2017. *Essentials of Contemporary Management*, 10th ed. New York, NY: McGraw-Hill Professional Publishing.

labor, and capital) into finished products and services that are competitive and meet the demands of customers with respect to utility, quality, and pricing; and management information systems ("MIS"), which focuses on collection, analysis, and dissemination of data and information regarding financial and operational activities of the organization.

Another theory, referred to as "systems management," emphasizes the importance of looking at organizations as "systems" with various interrelated parts that can be classified as inputs, transformation processes, outputs, and feedback. Systems management theory generally discusses and focuses on two types of systems: a "closed" system, which is an organization that has relatively little interaction with its external environment and thus gets little or no feedback and is at risk to suffer entropy, loses its ability to control itself and eventual dissolve; and an "open" system, which is an organization that interacts frequently with its external environment and thus receives information, feedback, and resources that can be used to make changes in transformation processes and outputs that are necessary in order for the organization to survive. Katz and Kahn were among the first to view organizations as open systems that appropriated resources (i.e., raw materials, capital and human resources) from their external environment, converted or transformed those resources into goods and services using appropriate tools and techniques, and then released those goods and services into the environment where they were purchased by customers to satisfy their needs. Money received from these purchases allowed the organization to acquire new resources that could be used to start the process again.[56]

Contingency School of Management

As the name implies, proponents of the contingency school of management believe that there is no single best way to manage and that what constitutes the most appropriate and effective management decision or action at a given time will depend on the situation that is confronting the

---

[56] Id. (citing Katz, D., and R. Kahn. 1966. *The Social Psychology of Organizations*, New York, NY: Wiley).

manager.[57] Managers acknowledging the contingency view have a good deal of flexibility; however, they also have a challenging task in figuring out which of the other various available theories of organizational design, control, and motivation offers the best solution. Under the contingency view, the experience, education, and judgment of the particular manager is extremely important for organizational effectiveness and managers must appreciate the potential influence of a diverse range of situational factors including type of organization, business purpose, and activities of the organization, size of the organization, operating environment, corporate and societal culture, information technology and communication, and, finally, the personal style and behavior of the owner or chief executive.

The rate of change in the organization's external environment is certainly an important contingency that managers need to take into account. Change can occur in a number of ways including the introduction of new technologies and products, entry of new competitors, and changes in overall economic conditions. Burns and Stalker, two of the pioneers in the development of contingency theory, argued that the optimal structure for an organization was related to the level of stability in the organization's external environment.[58] Organizations operating in a stable environment were likely to prefer a "mechanistic" structure based on Theory X management principles such as centralized authority, clearly defined tasks and rules, and close supervision. Jones and George explained that

[a] mechanistic structure provides the most efficient way to operate in a stable environment because it allows managers to obtain inputs at the lowest cost, giving an organization the most control over its conversion processes and enabling the most efficient production of goods and services with the smallest expenditure of resources.[59]

In contrast, managers of organizations that are operating in a rapidly changing and relatively unstable environment may be forced to

---

[57] Id.
[58] Id. See also Burns, T., and G.M. Stalker. 1961. *The Management of Innovation*. Oxford University Press.
[59] Id.

use an "organic" structure in which authority is decentralized and delegated downward in the hierarchy, roles are left ambiguous, employees are encouraged and expected to cooperate, and control is based not on fixed rules but on more informal shared norms for the conduct of organizational activities. Organic structures are better suited than mechanistic structures to cope with a turbulent environment; however, they are more expensive to operate and require new and different managerial skills.

Quality School of Management

The quality school of management focuses on "continuous improvement" of quality and performance to meet and exceed the needs and expectations of customers. Quality becomes the overriding priority for organizational activities and quality management techniques rely heavily on input from employees and close collaboration within the organization through teams of managers and employees that work together to set plans and identify and solve problems. Emphasis on quality management actually began during the era of Taylorism when researchers analyzed methods for controlling production and costs and acknowledged the need to attend to customer service as well as profits. As time went by, more and more work was done on statistical quality control and companies were urged to rely on internal customers and partnerships with suppliers in order to identify and resolve quality issues. Quality was an important element of emerging proposals for managerial priorities such as the system advocated by Deming, who is sometimes referred to as the "father of Quality," which included calls for managers to stop depending on inspections to achieve quality and focus instead on building quality into the product in the first place; continuously improve systems of production and service in order to improve quality and productivity and decrease costs; and break down barriers between departments to allow specialists in research, design, sales, and production to work as a team in order to foresee and resolve problems of production and use that may be encountered in connection with a product or service.[60]

---

[60] Deming, W. 1986. *Out of the Crisis*, 23–24. Cambridge, MA: Cambridge University Press.

Two well-known quality-based initiatives are the Kaizen (pronounced "ky-zen") and reengineering approaches. Imai has defined Kaizen as "ongoing improvement involving everyone—top management, managers, and workers"[61] and Kaizen is supported by organizational norms that value learning and experimenting with respect to ideas that might lead to changes that enhance the quality of organizational outputs. Kaizen has its roots in Japanese manufacturing processes and has been incorporated into a similar concept of total quality management (TQM), which Davenport has defined to include programs and initiatives that emphasize incremental improvement in work processes and outputs over an open-ended period of time. Jones and George explained that "TQM focuses on analyzing an organization's input, conversion, and output activities to increase product quality."[62]

Reengineering, on the other hand, has been defined by Davenport to include discrete initiatives intended to achieve radically redesigned and improved work processes in a bounded time frame.[63] Reengineering is sometime referred to as "business process redesign" or "process innovation" and requires participation by everyone in the organization to seek and achieve dramatic improvements in cost, quality, and service. Reengineering is often controversial given its cost and the potential disruption that may result due to the need to reconfigure jobs and eliminate workers.[64] In order for either of the quality management approaches to be successful, the organizational culture must create an environment in which all employees work together in harmony and seek to develop and maintain cooperative relationships with their peers and everyone above or below them in the organizational hierarchy. The assumptions and

---

[61] Imai, M. 1986. *KAIZEN: The Key to Japan's Competitive Success*, xxix. New York, NY: Random House Business Division.

[62] Jones, G., and J. George. 2017. *Essentials of Contemporary Management*, 10th ed. New York, NY: McGraw-Hill Professional Publishing.

[63] Davenport, T. 1993. *Process Innovation*. Boston, MA: Harvard Business School Press.

[64] Davenport, T. July 1994. "Reengineering: Business Change of Mythic Proportions?" *MIS Quarterly*, pp. 121–27.

values underlying this form of culture have been referred to by Ouchi as "Theory Z."[65]

Other Contributions to the Development of Management Studies

The foregoing brief history of the development of "management" necessarily omits much in the way of important detail and debate and cannot possibility capture the diversity of thought and scholarship on the topic. For example, when one seeks to learn about "management" he or she inevitably is drawn to the collective works of Peter Drucker, who began his career by publishing one of the earliest books on applied management in 1946 and eventually became known as the "creator and inventor of modern management" in the words of well-known management commentator Tom Peters.[66] The field of management studies has also been overtaken by a seemingly endless stream of "new ideas" for management systems and practices such as "management-by-objectives," Six Sigma and "agile" software development. In addition, various subareas of management have developed their own body of scholarship as evidenced by the work being done under the umbrellas of human resource management, marketing management, strategic management, and financial management. However, the utility of these function-based initiatives has been questioned by those who argue that effective management in the 21st century requires an understanding of all of these categories and thus it is best to focus on specific processes or objectives such as product development. Finally, while much of what has been described previously has been introduced in the for-profit arena, there is a substantial amount of interest in management of public enterprises, nonprofit organizations, and organizations seeking to achieve both financial sustainability and societal benefits (e.g., social entrepreneurship).

---

[65] See generally Ouchi, W. 1981. *Theory Z: How American Business Can Meet the Japanese Challenge*. Reading, MA: Addison-Wesley.

[66] Byrne, J. November 28. 2005. "The Man Who Invented Management: Why Peter Drucker's Ideas Still Matter." *Bloomberg Businessweek*.

One of the most striking developments over the last few decades has been the emergence of "management" as a formal business discipline with its own body of scholarly work and a wide array of professional activities among educators, researchers, and others. The notion that management is just "common sense" and "cannot be taught" has been replaced by a complex model of formal education that produces graduates who have completed a curriculum that spans a wide range of subtopics. The formalization of "management" training has been accompanied by the development of other related business specialties such as finance, marketing, operations management, and human resources. Accounting and economics also play an important role in organizational strategy and operations; however, they both had already been recognized as established professions before the managerial profession began its rise. Today, integration of management skills into the local population is seen as essential to potential prosperity for developing countries.

Managerial Challenges in the Early 21st Century

The governance structure of for-profit organizations, generally corporations, in the United States has evolved to the point where one can identify several layers of stakeholders: the shareholders, who provide the capital to operate the business in exchange for retaining the right to receive profits generated from such operations; the directors, who are elected by the shareholders to oversee the operations of the business; the senior managers, who are employed by the directors to establish and execute a strategic plan for the business and manage day-to-day operations; and the lower-level managers and employees who carry out the various tasks and activities necessary for the organization to pursue, and hopefully achieve, its goals and objectives. For-profit organizations seek to generate profits for the shareholders, which also increase the compensation for the senior managers; create and distribute products and services that are valued by customers such that they will pay the price sought by the organization; and, at least under contemporary theories of human resources, provide rewarding opportunities for employees. Some countries use somewhat different governance models that feature a higher level of employee participation in governance through opportunities to elect worker representatives to the governing body (i.e., the board of directors). There is also a growing trend toward requiring that the needs and concerns of other stakeholders, such as the community in which the organization is operating, be taken into account when setting goals for, and making decisions about, the organization.

The 21st century began with celebration of a "New Economy" in which many of the traditional tools upon which management studies had been based with no longer be valid and managers would be challenged to cope with a variety of issues arising out of rapid and sweeping changes in society and the economy. While it may not be wise or necessary to throw out all of the "old," it is certainly important to pay attention to the several important factors identified and discussed by manager scholars and researchers such as Lewis et al.: continuous advances in information technology; the rise of the Internet; increasing globalization; increasing diversity in the workplace and the marketplace; growing recognition of the importance of intellectual capital including, but not limited to, intellectual property; and more focused attention on ethical behavior by firms and their managers.[67] Each of these factors has had, and will continue to have, a significant influence on core managerial activities, notably each of the elements of organizational design. In addition, of course, management must remain focused on creating value for customers in an efficient manner and on developing and implementing strategies to attract necessary inputs such as capital, technology and human resources.

Internet and Information Technology

The maturation of the Internet and evolution of information technology has had a dramatic impact on management tools, strategies, and challenges. After an initial period of colossal failures, including the so-called Internet bust at the beginning of the new century, the success rate of e-businesses finally began to rise as companies realized how they could develop business tools and strategies that had traditionally been practiced

---

[67] Lewis, P., S. Goodman, P. Fandt, and J. Michlitsch. 2007. *Management: Challenges for Tomorrow's Leaders*, 12–16, 5th ed. Mason, OH: Thomson South-Western.

in the pre-Internet world: operational efficiencies, cost containment, and control and intelligently designed strategic alliances. Concurrently, "brick-and-mortar" companies began to figure how they could use the Internet to compliment, rather than replace, their existing businesses, which meant that consumers began to have real choices about where and how they could purchase products and services and how they could communicate with their preferred vendors. Improvements in information technology facilitate rapid dissemination of information within organizations and efficient broadcast of information to the marketplace. Information technology also supports strong supply chain relationships, which, in turn, allow companies to reduce costs and improve service and product availability. Finally, there is no doubt that the Internet has changed the competitive landscape for businesses of all sizes: consumers can get more information about products, services, and vendors and can "comparison shop" quickly and efficiently; consumers can share information about their experiences with products, services, and vendors through social networking and, finally, competition can now arise from anywhere in the world where a person or firm can set up a website and ship products efficiently by taking advantage of improvements in logistics and transportation.[68]

Globalization

Businesses and their managers have had to come to grips with the fact that they need to think "globally" when making decisions about organizational strategy and design. The importance of globalization has increased with advances in information technology and transportation and firms of all sizes can now easily reach to customers and business partners around the world. Larger companies in particular have decided to move major parts of their operations to foreign countries to take advantage of cost advantages, gain access to talent and technology, and have more direct contact with consumers in large emerging markets. Interestingly, manufacturing is just one of the activities happening in foreign countries and

---

[68] Lewis, P., S. Goodman, P. Fandt, and J. Michlitsch. 2007. *Management: Challenges for Tomorrow's Leaders*, 12–13, 5th ed. Mason, OH: Thomson South-Western.

companies have increasingly looked to foreign scientists and engineers to carry out sophisticated research and development projects. There has also been a steady rise in strategic alliances between companies in different countries including, in many cases, acquisitions of controlling interests in US companies by foreign firms. In addition, the domestic marketplace in the United States has been transformed by inbound investment by foreign firms interested in setting up manufacturing and sales subsidiaries in the United States to increase the efficiency of their efforts to penetrate the US market.[69] Finally, globalization means that countries all around the world are developing their own indigenous management practices that leverage their specific resources and core competencies and help to create powerful local firms that quickly capture domestic market share and make it difficult for foreign companies to enter and gain access to growing middle classes with disposable income.

Diversity

Communication and organizational culture are two key concerns for managers of all businesses and the challenges in both of these areas have increased as the workplace and consumer marketplace have each become more diverse. Immigration and shifts in societal ideas about the roles of women have transformed the labor force to a dynamic and complex mix of men, women, Caucasians, Hispanics, African Americans, Asian Americans, and others with diverse racial, national, and ethnic backgrounds. As a result, issues have arisen in achieving the consensus necessary to set and pursue common goals and objectives and creating and maintaining a strong organizational culture is a much more difficult task for managers. The response has been an increase in diversity training within organizations to provide everyone with a better understanding of the perspectives of others with different backgrounds. Workplace diversity matches changes in the marketplace and companies must take into account the specific preferences of each of the aforementioned groups when designing and marketing their products and services.[70]

---

[69] Id. at 13.

[70] Id. at 13–14.

Intellectual Capital

Intellectual capital has joined the traditional factors of land, labor, money, and raw materials as essential contributors to the efficiency and competitiveness of business organizations and managers must have a clear understanding of the elements of intellectual capital and how they can be used in developing and implementing strategies. Intellectual capital appears in the growing sophistication and educational background of the workforce and in the nature of the products and services developed and marketed by business organizations. As noted by Lewis et al.,

> More and more products will become intellectual, or knowledge-based (for example, investment services and advice, registering for classes at a school, computer software), and may be better referred to as services. Services such as travel and entertainment are becoming more important, and they rely on knowledge. Even the traditional products will make more use of knowledge in design, production and marketing of them.[71]

Intellectual capital does not simply mean technology and intellectual property rights; instead, it is a concept that is much broader and includes identification, categorization, protection, and effective use of the totality of the organization's "knowledge." The three major categories of "intellectual capital" identified by Stewart include structural capital, which includes the accumulated knowledge and know-how of the organization represented by its patents, trademarks, copyrights, trade secrets, and proprietary claims to information in its databases and systems; customer capital, which includes the value of established relationships with customers and suppliers; and human capital, which includes the cumulative skills and knowledge of the organization.[72] Management of intellectual capital is tightly aligned with human resource management since managers must

---

[71] Lewis, P., S. Goodman, P. Fandt, and J. Michlitsch. 2007. *Management: Challenges for Tomorrow's Leaders*, 14, 5th ed. Mason, OH: Thomson South-Western.
[72] Id. (citing Stewart, T. 1997. *Intellectual Capital: The New Wealth of Organizations*. New York, NY: Currency Doubleday).

recruit and retain the best talent, mine their knowledge for the benefit of the organization, and establish systems for ensuring that their knowledge is available to others and that they have access to all of the organizational intellectual capital that they need in order to successfully carry out their activities.

Ethics

Ethical behavior and social responsibility have become two important topics for managers, particularly in light of the scandals and difficult economic times that made their marks on the first decade of the new century.[73] Government regulations such as the Sarbanes Oxley Act of 2002 transformed the landscape for corporate governance of public companies in the United States, with a particular focus on greater disclosure and transparency, and ethical guidelines have been promulgated by respected groups around the world including the OECD Guidelines for Multinational Enterprises and the United Nations Norms on the Responsibilities of Transnational Corporations and Other Business Enterprises. Management concerns regarding compliance are no longer limited to their own organizations and are now being extended to business partners such as suppliers under laws and voluntary standards that call for firms to monitor their supply chains for evidence of human trafficking and subpar working conditions.

Another interesting development in the United States is the recognition of new legal forms of corporations that explicitly allow directors to consider not only the interests of shareholders but also other important stakeholders such as employees, consumers and the community. A number of states, including California and Delaware, permit the formation of "benefit corporations," sometimes referred to as "B corporations," for the purpose of creating general public benefit, which is defined by statute as a material positive impact on society and the environment, taken as a whole, as assessed against a third-party standard that satisfies certain requirements. Directors of benefit corporations are required to consider the impacts of any action or proposed action upon specified

---

[73] Id. at 15–16.

considerations including, among others, the shareholders and employees of the corporation, customers of the corporation who are beneficiaries of the general or specific public benefit purposes, and the environment. The viability of B corporations will depend in large part on the development of case law regarding the permissible purposes of such corporations and the flexibility afforded to directors in discharging their fiduciary duties.

CHAPTER 2

Cross-Cultural Studies of Management Practices

Introduction

While it has been argued that certain management practices and styles have universal appeal and effectiveness, the reality seems to be that there are real and significant differences between countries with respect to their business and innovation systems and their preferences regarding leadership and management styles. Berry et al. argued that these differences, which they referred to as "cross-national distance," were likely based on a wide range of factors and suggested and defined the following set of "dimensions of cross-national distance"[1]:

- Economic: Differences in economic development and macroeconomic characteristics
- Financial: Differences in financial sector development
- Political: Differences in political stability, democracy, and trade bloc membership
- Administrative: Differences in colonial ties, language, religion, and legal system
- Cultural: Differences in attitudes toward authority, trust, individuality, and importance of work and family
- Demographic: Differences in demographic characteristics
- Knowledge: Differences in patents and scientific production

[1] Berry, H., M.F. Guillen, and N. Zhou. December 2010. "An Institutional Approach to Cross-national Distance." *Journal of International Business Studies* 41, pp. 1460–80. Berry et al. also provided a bibliography of theoretical sources for each dimension in the institutional literature and examples of empirical studies on each dimension in the international business literature.

- Connectedness: Differences in tourism and Internet use
- Geographic: Great circle distance between geographic center of countries

It is reasonable to assume that each of the factors listed earlier will influence the styles and practices used by managers and the expectations of subordinates regarding the actions and behaviors of their managers; however, a number of management scholars have concluded that societal culture had the biggest impact on the management styles selected by organizations operating within a society. Research and proscriptions regarding culture and management began to emerge and proliferate as businesses around the world were exposed to globalization and their interactions with people and firms in other countries increased. One of the most popular topics was the transferability of management styles and practice across cultural divides including the transfer of Western management styles to developing countries and the feasibility of US managers importing the management practices of the Japanese firms that rose rapidly to global market leadership in the 1980s. While the initial assumption and hope was that management styles and practices could move easily and seamlessly from country to country, success was difficult to achieve. In that regard, Bigoness and Blakely commented that "[i]ncreasingly, researchers and practitioners are concluding that the exportability of management theories and practices is determined by the comparability of the cultural values between the exporting and importing nation" and also cited Erez for the proposition that "the congruence between (societal values and managerial practices) has increasingly been shown to influence organizational outcomes."[2]

It may be a bit extreme to assume that societal culture is the most important environmental factor affecting management functions, particularly given the evidence that has been collected about the influence of economic, political, and legal institutions on formation, operation, growth, and survival of businesses. Moreover, the choices that managers can reasonably make regarding strategies related to the various managerial

---

[2] Bigoness, W.J., and G. Blakely. 1996. "A Cross-National Study of Managerial Values." *Journal of International Business Studies* 27, no. 4, pp. 739–752, 739.

functions are constrained by available technological know-how and physical infrastructure and by sociocultural variables such as religion, education, and language. Nonetheless, societal culture, which itself is influenced by the factors mentioned previously and evolves as societies and the people within them adapt to changes in their external and internal environments, must be acknowledged as a fundamental consideration for managerial attitudes and behaviors. As explained by Deresky:

> As generally understood, the culture of a society comprises the shared values, understandings, assumptions, and goals that are learned from earlier generations, imposed by present members of a society, and passed on to succeeding generations. This shared outlook results, in large part, in common attitudes, codes of conduct, and expectations that subconsciously guide and control certain norms of behavior. ... These cultural variables, in turn, determine basic attitudes toward work, time, materialism, individualism, and change. Such attitudes affect an individual's motivation and expectations regarding work and group relations, and they ultimately affect the outcomes that can be expected from that individual.[3]

International Studies of Influence of Culture on Management Practices

Comparison of management styles and practices used and preferred in different countries is facilitated by cross-cultural studies of management practices and a large number of studies have tested and appeared to verify the argument that societal values do influence the selection and effectiveness of managerial practices. For example, Bigoness and Blakely provided references to a selected set of these studies that included the following[4]:

---

[3] Deresky, H. 2013. International Management: Managing across Borders and Cultures, Text and Cases, pp. 8th ed. pp. 91–92.

[4] Bigoness, W.J., and G. Blakely. 1996. "A Cross-National Study of Managerial Values." *Journal of International Business Studies* 27, no. 4, pp. 739–752, 739–741.

- Social loafing was found to be present in an individualistic society such as the United States but not in a collectivist society such as China.[5]
- A Likert System 2 ("benevolent authoritative") management style was preferred in Mexico while a Likert System 3 ("consultative") management style was preferred in the United States.[6]
- Extrinsic rewards and behavioral management were found to be effective with workers in Russian textile factories; however, the performance of those same workers noticeably declined when "participative" management techniques were introduced.[7]
- In a comparison of British and French managers, the British were found to place greater emphasis on individual achievement than their French counterparts while, in turn, the French placed greater importance on competent supervision, sound company policies, fringe benefits, security, and good working conditions.[8]
- Business school students in Australia were interested in extrinsic factors while business school students in the United States were more interested in self-fulfillment, responsibility, and other types of intrinsic rewards.[9]

---

[5] Earley, P.C. 1989. "Social Loafing and Collectivism." *Administrative Science Quarterly* 34, 556–581.

[6] Morris, T., and C. Pavett. 1992. "Management Style and Productivity in Two Cultures." *Journal of International Business Studies* 23, no. 1, pp. 169–179.

[7] Welsh, D., F. Luthans, and S. Sommer. 1993. "Managing Russian Factory Workers: The Impact of U.S.-based Behavioral and Participative Techniques." *Academy of Management Journal* 36, no. 1, pp. 58–79.

[8] Kanungo, R., and R. Wright. 1983. "A Cross-Cultural Comparative Study of Managerial Job Attitudes." *Journal of International Business Studies* 13, no. 2, pp. 115–29.

[9] Dowling, P., and T. Nagel. 1986. "Nationality and Work Attitudes: A Study of Australian and American Business Majors." *Journal of Management* 12, no. 1, pp. 121–28.

- American managers were found to value individuality while their Japanese counterparts placed greater emphasis on socially oriented qualities.[10]
- Profit-making was important in the decisions of successful managers in the United States, United Kingdom, and Germany while successful managers in Denmark were more interested in societal concerns during their decision-making processes.[11]
- Kuwaiti managers were more likely to make business decisions based on their personal goals than US managers.[12]
- While managers in Sweden showed little reluctance to bypass the hierarchical chain of command when they deemed it necessary their counterparts in Italy felt such an action was a serious offense calling for either discipline or adjusting the organizational structure.[13]

The sections that follow provide a small sample of the many cross-national studies of managerial styles and practices. Bigoness and Blakely conducted a cross-national study of instrumental managerial values involving managers in 12 developed countries and found that while there appeared to be universal support for the importance of several values— broadmindedness, capability, courage, imagination, independence, and intelligence—there were also differences among the countries in the level

---

[10] Howard, A., K. Shudo, and M. Umeshima. 1983. "Motivation and Values among Japanese and American Managers." *Personal Psychology* 36, no. 4, pp. 883–98.

[11] Bass, B.M., and L.D. Eldridge. 1973. "Accelerated Managers' Objectives in Twelve Countries." *Industrial Relations: A Journal of Economy and Society* 12, no. 2, pp. 158–71.

[12] Yasin, M.M., T. Zimmerer, and R.F. Green. 1989. "Cultural Values as Determinants of Executive Attitudes." *International Journal of Value-Based Management* 2, no. 2, pp. 35–47.

[13] Laurent, A. 1983. "The Cultural Diversity of Western Management Conceptions." *International Studies of Management and Organization* 8, nos. (1–2), pp. 75–96.

of importance that managers assigned to certain values.[14] Bigoness and Blakely also found evidence that societal culture seemed to have a role in explaining differences between managers from different countries with respect to technology transfer, organizational development, and negotiation techniques. Bloom and Van Reenen conducted an exhaustive international study of patterns of management and productivity based on interviews with managers in 17 countries and concluded that not only did firms with "better" management practices tend to perform better but that management practices varied tremendously across firms and countries and countries specialized in different styles of management.[15] In addition to large multicountry studies, researchers have shown a particular interest in comparing Western and Asian management styles and behaviors. For example, Weihrich compared management practices in the United States, Japan, and China using five dimensions: planning, organizing, staffing, leading, and controlling.[16] Culpan and Kucukemiroglu conducted a comparative study of management styles in the United States and Japan using their suggested "conceptual model of management style" that included six dimensions: supervisory style, decision-making process, communication patterns, control mechanisms, interdepartmental relationships, and paternalistic orientation.[17] Yu and Yeh also examined Asian and Western management styles and found evidence for differences on several different dimensions including control, decision making, leadership style, communication style, goal orientation, and motivational style.[18]

---

[14] Bigoness, W.J., and G. Blakely. 1996. "A Cross-National Study of Managerial Values." *Journal of International Business Studies* 27, no. 4, pp. 739–752, 739.

[15] Bloom, N., and J. Van Reenen. Winter 2010. "Why Do Management Practices Differ Across Firms and Countries." *Journal of Economic Perspectives* 24, no. 1, pp. 203–24.

[16] Weihrich, H. March/April 1990. "Management Practices in the United States, Japan and the People's Republic of China." *Industrial Management*, pp. 3–7.

[17] Culpan, R., and O. Kucukemiroglu. 1993. "A Comparison of US and Japanese Management Styles and Unit Effectiveness." *Management International Review* 33, pp. 27–42.

[18] Pei-Li Yu and Quey-Jen Yeh. N.d. "Asian and Western Management Styles, Innovative Culture and Professionals' Skills." http://scribd.com/doc/61439046/HR-Abstracts (accessed December 31, 2018).

Bigoness and Blakely's Cross-National Study of Managerial Values

Bigoness and Blakely conducted a cross-national study of managerial values by surveying 567 managers from 12 countries: Australia, Brazil, Denmark, France, Great Britain, Germany, Italy, Japan, the Netherlands, Norway, Sweden, and the United States. Using factor analysis of the 18 instrumental values included in Rokearch's Value Survey,[19] Bigoness and Blakely found the following four underlying value dimensions, which are presented and explained in the order of importance afforded to the dimensions by the countries in the survey[20]:

- Most Important: Broadminded, capable, and courageous instrumental values
- Second Most Important: Imaginative, independent, and intellectual instrumental values
- Third Most Important: Clean, obedient, polite, responsible, and self-control instrumental values
- Lowest Ranked in Importance: cheerful, forgiving, helpful, and loving instrumental values

Notable observations from the Bigoness and Blakely study included the following:

- Managers from all 12 countries ranked the four dimensions in the same order of importance, providing some support for those who argue managerial values around the world are becoming increasingly homogenous. In that same vein, no differences in the level of importance were found among

---

[19] Bigoness, W.J., and G.L. Blakely. 1996. "A Cross-National Study of Managerial Values." *Journal of International Business Studies* 27, no. 4, pp. 739–752, 739. With respect to the 18 instrumental values, see Rokeach, M. 1968. *Beliefs, Attitudes and Values: A Theory of Organization and Change.* San Francisco, CA: Jossey-Bass.

[20] Bigoness, W.J., and G.L. Blakely. 1996. "A Cross-National Study of Managerial Values." *Journal of International Business Studies* 27, no. 4, pp. 739–752, 748.

the surveyed countries with respect to the dimension that included imaginative, independent, and intellectual, leading Bigoness and Blakely to conclude that managers in all countries view these items as important values.[21]

- Japanese managers placed much greater emphasis than managers from the other countries on the dimension that included cheerful, forgiving, helpful, and loving. Bigoness and Blakely explained that this was consistent with the collectivist nature of Japanese societal culture and previous studies that had found that Japanese business culture valued cooperation, personalized and family-oriented managerial style, avoidance of public confrontation, and good work group relations and teamwork.[22]

- The dimension that included broadminded, capable, and courageous was seen as significantly less important by US managers in comparison to managers in seven other countries. Bigoness and Blakely noted that this was consistent with other studies that had shown that US managers were less interested in using personal influence and assertiveness-control and preferred using a dominating style that was inconsistent with being "broadminded."[23]

---

[21] Id. (citing also Elizur, D., I. Borg, R. Hunt, and I. Beck. 1991. "The Structure of Work Values: A Cross-Cultural Comparison." *Journal of Organizational Behavior* 12, no. 1, pp. 21–38). (agreement among workers in eight countries that achievement and performing interesting work were important motivating factors).

[22] Id. at 749 (citing Beer, M., S. Marsland, and B. Spector. 1981. "Note on Japanese Management and Employment Systems." *Harvard Business School Case Study*, pp. 9–48).

[23] Id. (citing also Whitely, W., and G. England. 1980. "Variability in Common Dimensions of Managerial Values due to Value Orientation and Country Differences." *Personal Psychology* 33, no. 1, pp. 77–78; and Ting-Toomey, S. 1988. "Intercultural Conflict Styles: A Face-Negotiation Theory." In *Theories in Intercultural Communication*, eds. Y.Y. Kim and W. Gudykunst, 213–235. Newbury Park, CA: Sage).

- The dimension that included clean, obedient, polite, responsible, and self-control was ranked significantly higher as favored by managers from Brazil and Japan than managers from Denmark, France, Great Britain, Italy, the Netherlands, Norway, and the United States. Bigoness and Blakely observed that it was interesting that managers from these two non-Western countries would place more importance of values based on "personal characteristics" than their colleagues in those seven Western countries. Of note, two Western countries, Australia and Germany, rated this dimension in the same way as Brazilian and Japanese managers.

The impact of differences in societal culture has also been measured and confirmed with respect to technology transfer, organizational development, and negotiation techniques.[24] On the other hand, however, there are studies that failed to find the expected national differences with respect to attitudes, work goals, or values.[25]

---

[24] Kedia, B.L., and R.S. Bhagat. 1988. "Cultural Constraints on the Transfer of Technology across Nations: Implications for Research in International and Comparative Management." *Academy of Management Review* 13, no. 4, pp. 559–71; Jaeger, A.M. 1986. "Organizational Development and National Culture: Where's the Fit?" *Academy of Management Review* 11, no. 1, pp. 178–90; and Shenkar, O., and S. Ronen. 1987. "The Cultural Context of Negotiation: The Implications of Chinese Interpersonal Norms." *Journal of Applied Behavioral Sciences* 23, no. 2, pp. 263–75.

[25] Harpaz, I. 1990. "The Importance of Work Goals: An International Perspective." *Journal of International Business Studies* 21, no. 1, pp. 75–93 (no significant difference in work values of workers from seven industrialized countries); Schwind, H.F., and R. Peterson. 1985. "Shifting Values in the Japanese Management System." *International Studies of Management and Organization* 15, no. 2, pp. 60–74. (Japanese students training to be managers in the United States had values more similar to US students than Japanese managers); and Ralston, D.A., D.J. Gustafson, P.M. Elsass, F. Cheung, and R.H. Terpstra. 1992. "Eastern Values: A Comparison of Managers in the United States, Hong Kong, and the People's Republic of China." *Journal of Applied Psychology* 77, no. 5, pp. 664–71 (greater individual variance than between-country variance in study of values of managers from the United States, Hong Kong, and China).

Bloom and Van Reenen's International Study of Patterns of Management

Bloom and Van Reenen completed an exhaustive international study of patterns of management and productivity based on almost 6,000 interviews conducted at large samples of firms in 17 countries: Australia, Brazil, Canada, China, France, Germany, Great Britain, Greece, India, Italy, Japan, Northern Ireland, Poland, Portugal, Republic of Ireland, Sweden, and the United States.[26] The number of firms from which observations were collected varied among the countries with the sample for the United States numbering 695 firms while the number of firms for Northern Ireland was 92. Firms were randomly selected and sampled from a pool of public and private manufacturing companies with 100 to 5,000 employees and Bloom and Van Reenen reported that the median firm in every country was privately owned, employed around 350 workers, and operated across two production plants. Bloom and Van Reenen relied on an interview-based evaluation tool that defined and scored from 1 ("worst practice") to 5 ("best practice") on the following 18 basic management practices or dimensions[27]:

1. Introduction of modern manufacturing techniques: What aspects of manufacturing have been formally introduced, including just-in-time delivery from suppliers, automation, flexible manpower, support systems, attitudes, and behavior?

2. Rationale for introduction of modern manufacturing techniques: Were modern manufacturing techniques adopted just because others were using them, or are they linked to meeting business objectives like reducing costs and improving quality?

---

[26] Bloom, N., and J. Van Reenen. Winter 2010. "Why Do Management Practices Differ Across Firms and Countries." *Journal of Economic Perspectives* 24, no. 1, pp. 203–24.

[27] Id. at 205–208 includes a discussion of the research methodology. See also Bloom, N., and J. Van Reenen. "New Approaches to Surveying Organizations." http://stanford.edu/~bloom/Surveying_AER.pdf A full set of questions for each dimension appears in Bloom, N., and J. Van Reenen. 2006. "Measuring and Explaining Management Practices across Firms and Countries." Centre for Economic Performance Discussion Paper 716.

3. Process problem documentation: Are process improvements made only when problems arise, or are they actively sought out for continuous improvement as part of a normal business process?

4. Performance tracking: Is tracking ad hoc and incomplete, or is performance continually tracked and communicated to all staff?

5. Performance review: Is performance reviewed infrequently and only on a success/failure scale, or is performance reviewed continually with an expectation of continuous improvement?

6. Performance dialogue: In review/performance conversations, to what extent is the purpose, data, agenda, and follow-up steps (like coaching) clear to all parties?

7. Consequence management: To what extent does failure to achieve agreed objectives carry consequences, which can include retraining or reassignment to other jobs?

8. Target balance: Are the goals exclusively financial, or is there a balance of financial and nonfinancial targets?

9. Target interconnection: Are goals based on accounting value, or are they based on shareholder value in a way that works through business units and ultimately is connected to individual performance expectations?

10. Target time horizon: Does top management focus mainly on the short term, or does it visualize short-term targets as a "staircase" toward the main focus on long-term goals?

11. Targets are stretching: Are goals too easy to achieve, especially for some "sacred cows" areas of the firm, or are the goals demanding but attainable for all parts of the firm?

12. Performance clarity: Are performance measures ill-defined, poorly understood, and private, or are they well-defined, clearly communicated, and made public?

13. Managing human capital: To what extent are senior managers evaluated and held accountable for attracting, retaining, and developing talent throughout the organization?

14. Rewarding high performance: To what extent are people in the firm rewarded equally irrespective of the performance level, or are rewards related to performance and effort?

15. Removing poor performers: Are poor performers rarely removed, or are they retrained and/or moved into different roles or out of the company as soon as the weakness is identified?

16. Promoting high performers: Are people promoted mainly on the basis of tenure, or does the firm actively identify, develop and promote its top performers?

17. Attracting human capital: Do competitors offer stronger reasons for talented people to join their companies, or does a firm provide a wide range of reasons to encourage talented people to join?

18. Retaining human capital: Does the firm do relatively little to retain top talent or do whatever it takes to retain top talent when they look likely to leave?

Bloom and Van Reenen assessed and ranked firms and countries on "overall management" by looking at the average score across all 18 questions or dimensions. In addition, they were interested in attempting to measure, rank, and compare the firms and countries on management practices in three broad areas: "monitoring management," which focused on how well managers monitor what goes on inside their firms and use this information for continuous improvement (evaluation and assessment of "monitoring management" was based on the average score across the aforementioned questions 1 to 6); "targets management," which focused on whether or not managers set the right targets for their firms, track the right outcomes for their firms, and then take appropriate action when targets and outcomes are inconsistent (evaluation and assessment of "targets management" was based on the average score across questions 8 to 12, listed earlier); and "incentives management," which focused on whether managers promoted and rewarded employees based on performance and trying to hire and keep their best employees (evaluation and assessment of "incentives management" was based on the average score across questions 7 and 13 to 18, shown previously).[28]

---

[28] Bloom and Van Reenen noted that the chosen areas were similar to those emphasized by other researchers such as Ichinowski, C., K. Shaw, and G. Prenushi. 1997. "The Effects of Human Resource Management: A Study of Steel Finishing Lines." *American Economic Review*, pp. 291–313; and Black, S., and L. Lynch. 2001. "How to Compete: The Impact of Workplace Practices and Information Technology on Productivity." *Review of Economics and Statistics* 83, no. 3, pp. 434–45. They also noted the work of Bertrand and Schoar that focused

The key finding from the Bloom and Van Reenen study was that firms with "better" management practices tend to have better performance on a wide range of dimensions: they were larger, more productive, grow faster, and have higher survival rates.[29] They also found that management practices varied tremendously across firms and countries and firms and countries "specialized" in different styles of management (e.g., firms in the United States scored much higher than firms in Sweden with respect to use of incentives; however, Swedish firms relied more heavily on monitoring than their counterparts in the United States).[30] Other interesting findings that transcended the borders of the countries included in the survey included confirmation that strong product market competition appeared to boost average management practices; that firms that exported into foreign markets, but did not manufacture in foreign markets, were better managed than those firms who stayed home and neither exported into or manufactured in foreign markets; and firms that were more reliant on human capital, as measured by the percentage of educated workers, tended to have much better management practices.

With respect to "overall management," firms in the US sample had the highest scores on average among the 17 countries: 3.33, compared to an average country score of 2.94.[31] The next group consisted of four countries: Germany, Sweden, Japan, and Canada, with scores ranging from 3.18 to 3.13. The third group included a block of mid-European countries (i.e., France, Italy, Ireland, Great Britain, and Poland) and Australia, with scores ranging from 3.00 to 2.84. Southern European countries such as Greece and Portugal, as well as Brazil, China, and India from the developing world, were in the bottom tier, with Greece and India scoring 2.65.

---

on the management styles of chief executive and chief financial officers and thus provided insight into another area, "strategic management," which is particular relevant for managers at the top of the organizational hierarchy. See Bertrand, M., and A. Schoar. 2003. "Managing with Style: The Effect of Managers on Firm Policies." *Quarterly Journal of Economics*, pp. 1169–208.

[29] Bloom, N., and J. Van Reenen. Winter 2010. "Why Do Management Practices Differ across Firms and Countries." *Journal of Economic Perspectives* 24, no. 1, pp. 203–224, 204.

[30] Id. at 205.

[31] Id.

Bloom and Van Reenen pointed out that most of the difference in the average management score of a country is due to the size of the "long tail" of very badly managed firms and cautioned that while Brazil and India, for example, had many firms in that category one could also find a number of well-managed firms in those countries.

Scores with respect to "incentives management" ranged from a high of 3.30 (United States) to a low of 2.50 (Greece) and the average was 2.84.[32] The US score was substantially higher than any of the other countries (Canada was second at 3.02 followed closely by Germany at 2.95) and over half of the countries fell within a narrow range between 2.75 and 2.90. Scores with respect to "monitoring management" ranged from a high of 3.54 (Sweden) to a low of 2.62 (India) and the average was 3.09. The United States (3.44) and Germany (3.40) were placed second and third with respect to this type of management, while countries such as Brazil (2.81), China (2.72), Greece (2.90), and Poland (2.88) scored near the bottom. Scores with respect to "targets management" ranged from a high of 3.25 (Japan) to a low of 2.53 (China) and the average was 2.91. However, while Japan had the highest score it was closely followed at the top of the ranking by Germany (3.24), the United States (3.23), and Sweden (3.22). In addition to China, poor performers with respect to this type of management included Brazil (2.68), Greece (2.56), India (2.66), and Portugal (2.72).

Patterns of management "specialization," or preferences for emphasizing particular types of management practices, could also be observed. For example, Bloom and Van Reenen noted:

> In the United States, India, and China, managerial use of incentives (relative to the average country) are substantially greater than their use of monitoring and targets (relative to the average). However, in Japan, Sweden, and Germany, managerial use of monitoring and targets (relative to the average) far exceeds their use of incentives (relative to the average).[33]

---

[32] Id.

[33] Id.

Bloom and Van Reenen speculated that the preference of US managers to use incentives was due, in part, to "lighter" labor market regulations in the United States that made it relatively easier for firms to terminate underperforming workers without substantial penalties and provide rewards to highly performing workers.

Weihrich's Comparative Study of United States, Japanese, and Chinese Management

Weihrich compared management practices in the United States, Japan, and China as of the late 1980s by looking at five dimensions often recognized as the key managerial functions: planning, organizing, staffing, leading, and controlling.[34] At the time, Weihrich noted that one of his primary goals was to determine whether US and/or Japanese managerial practices would be appropriate for Chinese businesses and he acknowledged that while a good deal of research had already been done on US and Japanese management, very little information was then available on Chinese management and what was available drew primarily from practices in large, state-owned businesses in China. He also cautioned that his profiles of predominant management practices were suggestive based on a review of the available literature and that other research results for the United States and Japan often invited and supported interpretations that were different from what Weihrich reported. For example, while Weihrich, like many others, noted differences between the United States and Japan with respect to worker participation in decision-making, there have been researchers who have found no differences between those countries. Weihrich also pointed out that external factors likely played a big role in differences between managerial styles in the three countries. Specifically, US managers were heavily influenced by pressure from shareholders to achieve "results" measured by short-term financial performance, Japanese managers operated in an environment in which the government was a close and important partner with respect to planning,

---

[34] Weihrich, H. March/April 1990. "Management Practices in the United States, Japan and the People's Republic of China." *Industrial Management*, pp. 3–7.

and Chinese managers had little or no experience with operating in the "private sector."

Culpan and Kucukemiroglu's Study of US and Japanese Management Styles

Culpan and Kucukemiroglu conducted a comparative study of management styles in the United States and Japan using their suggested "conceptual model of management style" that included the following six dimensions[35]:

- Supervisory style, which refers to the different ways that supervisors act during their interactions with their subordinates and to the different styles that supervisors use in order to relate to their subordinates (e.g., task versus relationship orientation and "participative" versus "autocratic");
- Decision-making process, which refers to the way in which decisions are made within an organizational unit and the extent to which subordinates contribute to or participating in managerial decisions;
- Communication patterns, which cover the functions of organizational communication, including providing informational input to decisions; establishing tasks, duties, roles, responsibilities, and authority; achieving cooperation, and guiding action toward goals; instructing, developing, and changing; and providing feedback;
- Control mechanisms, which refer to the comparison of strategic goals and standards with outcomes and the processes that supervisors use to check on the conduct of operational activities to determine whether the results achieved by subordinates in carrying out those activities meet the performance goals and standards established by the organization;

---

[35] Culpan, R., and O. Kucukemiroglu. 1993. "A Comparison of US and Japanese Management Styles and Unit Effectiveness." *Management International Review* 33, pp. 27–42.

- Interdepartmental relationships, which focuses on the degree of interaction among departments within an organization and the ability of departments to obtain the inputs from other departments (e.g., resources, services and/or information) that they require in order to accomplish their own departmental objectives; and
- Paternalistic orientations, which measures the level of managerial concern with the personal and family life of subordinates and the amount of effort invested by managers in providing social support for subordinates.

Data was collected using a questionnaire from top and middle managers from manufacturing firms in the United States and Japan—US firms were randomly selected from manufacturers operating in New York, New Jersey, and Pennsylvania while the Japanese companies were randomly selected from the *Japan Company Handbook 1989*. Four questionnaires were mailed to each Japanese company. In general, companies in the sample were medium- and large-sized manufacturing firms. The results of their survey confirmed their hypotheses that management styles as defined using these dimensions differed significantly between the United States and Japan and that managers in each country considered each dimension differently and emphasized different sets of managerial dimensions: Japanese managers placed the most emphasis on communication pattern, interdepartmental relations, and paternalistic orientation while US managers focused on supervisory style, decision-making, and control mechanism. They also found that Japanese managers considered their business units to be more "effective" than their counterparts in the United States.

Culpan and Kucukemiroglu commented that their results confirmed earlier theories and findings regarding comparisons of US and Japanese management systems, including the works of Ouchi, Pascale, and Hatvany and Pucik.[36] They observed that communications in Japanese

---

[36] Culpan, R., and O. Kucukemiroglu. 1993. "A Comparison of US and Japanese Management Styles and Unit Effectiveness." *Management International Review* 33, pp. 27–42. (citing Hatvany, N., and V. Pucik. 1981. "An Integrated

firms appeared "to be open and mostly face-to-face thereby minimizing barriers to effective information flow" and that Japanese managers paid particular attention to interactions between departments and "interdepartmental dependency and cooperation." The openness of communications provided support for the strong feelings among Japanese managers that their units operated effectively. In contrast, US management systems as that time were described as "mostly characterized by supervisory style stressing more Theory X type, task-oriented, and transactional leadership methods", and it was noted that US managers were more interested in results than processes, tended to be less participatory than Japanese managers with respect to decision-making (i.e., "top-down" decision making was the norm in the United States) and relied on "a control mechanism based on close supervision and an explicit formal control pattern."[37] The paternalistic orientation in Japan was clearly a distinguishing factor between the two countries and the study provided further evidence for the long understood belief that Japanese firms and managers were especially attentive to the concerns and activities of employees outside of the workplace. Culpan and Kucukemiroglu took specific note of the fact that in all three managerial processes specifically associated with the predominant practices of Japanese managers, "the key to the success seems to be the management style encouraging employee involvement."[38]

Culpan and Kucukemiroglu also argued that managerial practices with respect to each of the dimensions should be evaluated against the prevailing norms and values of the societal culture in which those practices were occurring and that managers should make the effort to modify their styles and practices to achieve a closer alignment with the cultural norms and values of their society. In the United States, for example,

---

Management System: Lessons from the Japanese Experience." *Academy of Management Review* 6, pp. 469–80; Pascale, R. 1978. "Communications and Decision-making: Cross-cultural Comparisons." *Administrative Science Quarterly* 23, pp. 91–110; and Ouchi, W. 1981. *Theory Z: How Can American Business Meet the Japanese Challenge*. Reading, MA: Addison-Wesley).

[37] Culpan, R., and O. Kucukemiroglu. 1993. "A Comparison of US and Japanese Management Styles and Unit Effectiveness." *Management International Review* 33, pp. 27–42.

[38] Id.

they observed that managers should emphasize democracy rather than authoritarianism with respect to their supervisory/leadership style given the great weight given to democratic values in American society and they suggested that US managers adopt transformational leadership virtues.[39] With regard to decision making, Culpan and Kucukemiroglu recommended that US managers integrate their subordinates into the process and accept more employee involvement and participation in management decision making as a means for increase employment commitment and morale and improving the performance of business units.[40] While it is not strictly necessary that employees have a "vote," managers should make an effort to regularly consult with employees before making their decisions and ensure that employees feel that they have been given a "fair hearing." If this approach is followed, the likelihood that employees will accept and follow a manager's decision, even one with which they do not agree, is increased.[41] Finally, Culpan and Kucukemiroglu believed that "an effective control technique for American organizations might entail incorporation of employee involvement with explicit control" and noted the apparent success of techniques such as "management by objectives"[42] and "goal setting"[43] in the United States. They reasoned that this approach would tap into the desire of US employees to assume responsibility for

---

[39] Tichy, N., and D. Ulrich. 1984. "The Leadership Challenge—A Call for the Transformational Leader." *Sloan Management Review* 26, no. 1, pp. 59–60.

[40] With regard to a similar impact on employee commitment and unit performance among Japanese firms, see Hatvany, H., and V. Pucik. 1981. "An Integrated Management System: Lessons from the Japanese Experience." *Academy of Management Review* 6, no. 3, pp. 469–80.

[41] See Rohlen, T. 1974. *For Harmony and Strength: Japanese White-collar Organization in Anthropological Perspective*, 308. Berkeley, CA: University of California Press. (managers should not "… decide until others who will be affected have had sufficient time to offer their views, feel they have been fairly heard, and are willing to support the decision even though they may not feel it's the best one").

[42] Drucker, P. 1954. *The Practice of Management*. New York, NY: Harper; and Carroll, S.J., and H.L. Tosi. 1973. *Management by Objectives: Application and Research*. New York, NY: Macmillan.

[43] Locke, E.A., and G. Latham. 1984. *Goal Setting: A Motivational Technique that Works*. Englewood Cliffs, NJ: Prentice-Hall.

necessary corrective actions while ensuring that they have clearly defined goals and standards to direct their work.

Yu and Yeh's Comparison of Asian and Western Management Styles

Yu and Yeh also examined differences between Asian and Western management styles and did so using the following dimensions[44]:

- Control: Asian style was described as hierarchical while elements of Western style included contracts and due diligence, flatter organizational structures, and more decentralization.
- Decision making: Asian decision-making style was centralized with a single decision maker while Western style was more corporate- or group-based.
- Leadership: Asian leadership style characterized as paternalistic, relationship-based, authoritarian, and directive while Western leadership style tended to be more participative.
- Communication: Asian communication style focused on deal orientation and the human side of relationships and personal behavior while Western communication style was characterized as "function-oriented."
- Goals: Asian management style emphasized harmony while Western style was more process-oriented.
- Motivation: Asian management style tended to follow collectivist values while Western management style followed individualistic values.
- Power Distance: Power distance among Asian societies was higher than among Western societies, which influenced attitudes regarding organizational structure, control, and decision making.

---

[44] Pei-Li Yu and Quey-Jen Yeh. N.d. "Asian and Western Management Styles, Innovative Culture and Professionals' Skills." http://www.scribd.com/doc/61439046/HR-Abstracts (accessed December 31, 2018).

Cross-Cultural Comparisons of Dimensions of Managerial Activities

In order for managers to learn from the results of cross-cultural studies of managerial styles and practices, it is useful to present those results in a way that matches the actual issues and activities that managers must deal with on a day-to-day basis and this approach was taken when organizing the following sections. Ideas were borrowed from many sources beginning with the five popular dimensions used in Weihrich's comparative study of management practices in the United States, Japan, and China that was described earlier: planning, organizing, staffing, leading, and controlling.[45] Five of the six dimensions included by Culpan and Kucukemiroglu in their suggested "conceptual model of management style" were integrated into Weihrich's five categories—"interdepartmental relationships" as important factors for effective "organizing," "supervisory style," "communication patterns," and "paternalistic orientation" as elements of "leading," and "control mechanisms" as means of "controlling"—and the remaining dimension, "decision-making processes," is presented separately since it is an area that has attracted a good deal of its own focused research interest.[46]

In addition to the dimensions used by Weihrich and Culpan and Kucukemiroglu, consideration was given to the suggestion of Nigam and Su that in order to understand management culture, reference should be made to the human resource management policies and practices observed to be in use during the day-to-day operations of the organization.[47] Human resources practices, and the activities of the human resources department, have often been recognized as important drivers of

---

[45] Weihrich, H. March/April 1990. "Management Practices in the United States, Japan and the People's Republic of China." *Industrial Management*, pp. 3–7.

[46] Culpan, R., and O. Kucukemiroglu. 1993. "A Comparison of US and Japanese Management Styles and Unit Effectiveness." *Management International Review* 33, pp. 27–42.

[47] Nigam, R., and Z. Su. 2011. "Management in Emerging versus Developed Countries: A Comparative Study from an Indian Perspective." *Journal of CENTRUM Cathedra* 4, no. 1, pp. 121–33, 122.

organizational performance.[48] While discussing the challenges confronting developing countries with respect to economic progress and integration into the global economy, Tabassi and Baker commented that

> with rapid changes in technology, worker's needs, current market, and competitive environment, planning for human resources has become an important and challenging task for development.[49]

One of the fundamental responsibilities for human resource departments is the development of knowledge and expertise among the workforce. In their framework for analyzing Indian management culture, Nigam and Su decided to focus on four dimensions, each of which were related to human resources management practices: power delegation; compensation, promotion, and rewards; performance appraisal; and training, development, and career planning.[50] In the sections that follow "power delegation" has been incorporated with other research on "decision making" and the other three dimensions in the Nigam and Su model were included in a discussion of how managers operating in different societal cultures seek to effectively motivate their subordinates.

Planning

The criteria used by Weihrich to compare planning processes included the relative weight given to short- versus long-term planning, the level of participation or involvement by persons at lower levels of the organizational hierarchy, whether decisions were made by one individual at the top of the hierarchy or by consensus or committee, the flow of the

---

[48] Woodard, N., and D. Saini. 2006. "Diversity Management Issues in USA and India: Some Emerging Perspectives." In *Future of Work: Mastering Change.* eds. P. Singh, J. Bhatnagar and A. Bhandarker, New Delhi, India: Excel Books.

[49] Tabassi, A.A., and A. Bakar. 2009. "Training, Motivation, and Performance: The Case of Human Resource Management in Construction Projects in Mashhad, Iran." *International Journal of Project Management* 27, no. 5, pp. 471–80.

[50] Nigam, R., and Z. Su. 2011. "Management in Emerging versus Developed Countries: A Comparative Study from an Indian Perspective." *Journal of CENTRUM Cathedra* 4, no. 1, pp. 121–33, 126.

decision-making process and the speed of decision making and implementation.[51] Weihrich argued that planning activities by US managers tended to be primarily oriented toward short-term goals and objectives and decisions were generally made solely by the person at the top of the organizational hierarchy and communicated downward. While this approach permitted fast decision making, it often hampered implementation since persons responsible for implementing decisions had not been involved at the outset and time had to be spent "selling" decisions to those persons, who often had divergent values. Implementation could lead to suboptimal results without the participation of subordinates in decision making due to the need to make compromises in order to secure the support of those subordinates. In contrast, Weihrich observed that Japanese managers had a long-term orientation with respect to planning and setting goals and objectives and collective decision-making processes were used to solicit input and achieve consensus among both managers and workers. Decision flow was from bottom-to-top and then back down once again and while the involvement of many people in the decision-making process tended to slow down that process it was believed that allowing workers to participate would ultimately smooth and quicken implementation of decisions. With respect to China, Weihrich found a mix of long- and short-term orientation with respect to planning as managers formulated both five-year plans with long-term objectives and annual plans that focused on the immediate operational goals that needed to be achieved in order to achieve the long-term objectives. Decision making occurred within committees although final decisions were generally made at the top of the organizational hierarchy by a single individual. Ideas were generated from the top and input was solicited from lower levels. In general, decision making tended to be slow and implementation was also relatively slow even though there was input from workers and it appeared that slow implementation followed from the fact that worker participation was not treated as seriously as in Japan.

---

[51] Weihrich, H. March/April 1990. "Management Practices in the United States, Japan and the People's Republic of China." *Industrial Management*, pp. 3–7.

Organizing

The criteria used by Weihrich to compare organizing practices included an assessment of whether responsibility and accountability was individualistic or collectivist, the degree of formality in the organizational structure, the level of clarity in decision-making responsibilities, and the strength of organizational culture.[52] Weihrich noted that organizational structures used by US managers tended to rely on individual responsibility and accountability and those managers preferred formal bureaucratic organizational structures with clear and specific rules and expectations about where decision-making responsibility lied. Weihrich argued that organizational culture was relatively weak in the United States compared to Japan and China and managers and workers often had stronger identifications with their profession than with their firms. In contrast, Weihrich observed that organizational structures in Japan were based relatively informal in comparison to the United States and based on collective responsibility and accountability. As a result, there tended to be ambiguity within the organization regarding decision-making responsibilities; however, this was mitigated to some degree by a strong and well-known common organizational culture and philosophy that aided everyone in grasping the "right thing to do" when confronted with operational decisions. Weihrich also observed that Japanese firms tended to have a strong competitive spirit toward other enterprises, which presumably contributed to a strong sense of collective responsibility and cooperation and collaboration in pursuing the goals and objectives of the firm. In addition, Weihrich reported that organizational structures in China tended to be formal and bureaucratic, although one found a mix of collective and individual responsibility and there had been attempts to introduce a "factory responsibility system" that delegated more authority to individual factories and even allowed them to pursue and generate profits at the factory level. Like Japan, organizational culture was strong in China; however, Chinese firms had yet to develop the competitiveness with other enterprises found in Japan.

---

[52] Id.

Another aspect of the managerial function of organizing is defining, creating, and maintaining "interdepartmental relationships," which Culpan and Kucukemiroglu explained to include the "degree of interaction among departments within an organization" and the ability of departments to obtain the inputs from other departments (e.g., resources, services, and/or information) that they require in order to accomplish their own departmental objectives.[53] Interdepartmental relationships can be regulated through formal rules and policies; however, day-to-day interaction between departments generally includes bargaining, exchange of favors, and communication regarding coordination. One suggested measure of the quality and effectiveness of interdepartmental relationships is the level of conflict with other departments and volume of criticism from other departments for failure of the department to be cooperative. In their comparative study of US and Japanese managers, Culpan and Kucukemiroglu found that interdepartmental interactions were more intensive in Japanese companies than in US companies and that managers in Japan paid more attention to issues relating to interdepartmental dependency and cooperation by, for example, encouraging open communications between departments consistent with Japanese culture preferences for group consultation and decision making.

Staffing

The criteria used by Weihrich to compare staffing practices included procedures for recruiting new employees, factors influencing speed of promotion, performance assessment, training and development, and security of employment.[54] Weihrich reported that US firms recruited both from schools and from other firms and employees tended to be more loyal to their professions than their employers and thus were likely to change firms frequently during the course of their careers. United States employees had high expectations with regard to rapid advancement and were subject to frequent performance evaluations with a focus on progress toward attainment of short-term results. Promotions in US firms were

---

[53] Id.

[54] Id.

based primarily on individual performance and US firms were reluctant to invest significantly in training and development of employees due to concerns that they would leave and take the skills that they have learned to competitors. The absence of "lifetime employment" expectations in the United States led to high levels of job insecurity. In Japan, according to Weihrich, most new employees were hired directly from school and Japanese employees were intensely loyal to their companies, resulting in low mobility between firms. The traditional expectation of lifetime employment, although eroding, had a substantial impact on the career paths of Japanese employees. Slow promotion was expected and newer employees received little or no feedback during their early careers. When feedback was provided it focused on appraisal of long-term performance and training and development was seen as a long-term investment. Weihrich found that Chinese firms tended to rely more heavily on schools than on other firms as sources of new employees and Chinese workers had little loyalty to their firms or their profession. Performance reviews were infrequent, typically annually, and while workers typically received regular salary increases the path for promotion was relatively slow. While promotions were supposed to be based on performance, potential ability, and education, the reality was that family ties and good relations with top managers were extremely important for advancement. Like their firms, Chinese workers had their own long- and short-term goals and objectives with respect to training and development. Chinese managers themselves were beginning to get more training in preparation for examinations organized by the state.

Leading

The criteria used by Weihrich to compare leadership practices of managers in the United States, Japan, and China included the preferred leadership style (e.g., directive or paternalistic), an assessment of the manager's role with respect to leadership of the group, attitudes toward confrontation and group harmony, and the flow of communication.[55] According to Weihrich, the leadership style relied upon by managers in the United

---

[55] Id.

States tended to be strong and directive with the senior manager acting as the decision maker and communications flowing top-down. Individualism complicated the task of managers as leaders in the United States and face-to-face confrontations were common as leaders attempted to clarify their decisions and expectations. In contrast, Japanese managers and workers preferred a paternalistic style and Japanese managers saw themselves as members of the group with a responsibility to guide communications and interaction within the group. Leading Japanese managers emphasized on cooperation and harmony, sought to avoid confrontation, and encouraged bottom-up communication. As for Chinese managers, Weihrich reported that they led as the head of committees responsible for setting goals and objectives and making decisions. While Chinese managers did use a directive style, and communication was generally top-down, they sought to avoid confrontation and maintain harmony among their subordinates.

Culpan and Kucukemiroglu were interested in describing and comparing the "supervisory styles" of US and Japanese managers, a task that called for an analysis of the different ways that managers acted during their interactions with their subordinates and to the different styles that managers used in order to relate to their subordinates. Culpan and Kucukemiroglu argued that some of the elements that might be analyzed in identifying and assessing supervisory style include the amount of discretion given to subordinates (e.g., did the managers insist on handling all work problems or did he or she allow subordinates to work out certain issues on their own), the degree of delegation of authority by managers to their subordinates (i.e., how much direction came from the manager at the top of the hierarchy), solicitation of inputs and opinions from subordinates, the freedom of subordinates to schedule their own work, the manager's sacrifice for his or her employees, whether supervision was "democratic" or "close," and the relationship of the manager's behavior to the expectations of subordinates that their efforts will result in desired rewards.

Culpan and Kucukemiroglu found that supervisory style was more often emphasized by US managers than Japanese managers and that the particular style preferred by US managers stressed on "Theory X type, task-oriented and transactional leadership methods." Culpan and Kucukemiroglu noted that US managers were more interested in results than processes, tended to be less participatory than Japanese managers with respect to decision making (i.e., "top-down" decision making was the norm in the United States), and relied on "a control mechanism based on close supervision and an explicit formal control pattern."[56] They also observed that Japan's strong "paternalistic orientation," which they defined as "managers' concern with personal and family life of employees and providing social support for them,"[57] was clearly a distinguishing factor between management practices in the United States and Japan and that there was substantial evidence to support the belief that Japanese firms and managers were especially attentive to the concerns and activities of employees outside of the workplace and providing employees with help on nonwork-related matters.[58]

Supervisory styles have been integral parts of several important leadership and management theories including McGregor's Theory X, which was based on "close supervision," and Theory Y, which featured "participative management" as the preferred supervisory style[59]; Likert's four systems of management, which ranged from "exploitive authoritative" (System 1) to his preferred approach of "participative" (System 4)[60]; and Fiedler and Chemers' distinction between task- and relationship-motivated supervisory approaches.[61] Supervisory style is also important in the "path-goal theory of leadership," which measures the effectiveness of a leader or manager by his or her ability to motivate and satisfy subordinates so they

[56] Culpan, R., and O. Kucukemiroglu. 1993. "A Comparison of US and Japanese Management Styles and Unit Effectiveness." *Management International Review* 33, pp. 27–42.

[57] Id.

[58] Culpan, R., and O. Kucukemiroglu. 1993. "A Comparison of US and Japanese Management Styles and Unit Effectiveness." *Management International Review* 33, pp. 27–42.

[59] McGregor, D. 1960. *The Human Side of Enterprise.* New York, NY: McGraw-Hill.

[60] Likert, R. 1961. *New Patterns of Management.* New York, NY: McGraw-Hill. In Likert's model, System 2 was "benevolent authoritative" and System 3 was "consultative."

[61] Fiedler, F., and M. Chemers. 1974. *Leadership and Effective Management.* Glenview, IL: Scott, Foresman.

will perform at the level required by the organization.[62] While Bass has been more widely cited for his views on leadership, his "transformational" leadership approach calls for development of styles and behaviors that motivate subordinates to perform beyond their own expectations.[63]

Another aspect of how managers led their subordinates that interested Culpan and Kucukemiroglu was how the managers designed and administered the functions or organizational communication, or "communication pattern," within their business unit including "providing informational input to decisions; establishing tasks, duties, roles, responsibilities, and authority; achieving cooperation, and guiding action toward goals; instructing, developing, and changing; and providing feedback."[64] Of particular interest with respect to this dimension was the flow of information within organizations and between departments and the identification of barriers to the flow of information. Indicators of free flow of information include the manager's awareness of unit performance and activities that were occurring within the unit, the ease with which subordinates could get their opinions and complaints in front of top management, and evidence that managers had ready access to the information that they needed in order to make decisions. In turn, a lack of awareness among subordinates of changes in policies and directions was a "red flag" of communication problems. It appears fairly clear that effective communications and clear flows of information are important conditions to effective organizational management.[65] Culpan and Kucukemiroglu found that communication patterns were given greater weight by Japanese managers in comparison to their counterparts in the United States and observed that communications in Japanese firms appeared "to be open and mostly face-to-face thereby minimizing barriers to effective

[62] House, R.J., and T.R. Mitchell. 1974. "Path-Goal Theory of Leadership." *Journal of Contemporary Business* 3, no. 4, pp. 81–97.

[63] Bass, B.M. 1985. *Leadership and Performance beyond Expectations.* New York, NY: Free Press.

[64] Culpan, R., and O. Kucukemiroglu. 1993. "A Comparison of US and Japanese Management Styles and Unit Effectiveness." *Management International Review* 33, pp. 27–42.

[65] See, e.g., Lewis. P. 1975. *Organization Communications: Essence of Effective Management.* Columbus, OH: Grid.

information flow" and that Japanese managers paid particular attention to interactions between departments and "interdepartmental dependency and cooperation." Culpan and Kucukemiroglu noted that Pascale had also found an extensive level of face-to-face communications in Japanese firms.[66]

Controlling

The criteria used by Weihrich to compare control practices included the locus of control (i.e., senior manager/group leader or peers), focus of control (i.e., individual or group performance), the importance of placing blame or "saving face," and the use of group improvement strategies such as quality control circles.[67] He argued that US managers tended to rely on formal control rules and procedures formulated and disseminated at the top of the organizational hierarchy and focusing on individual performance to identify persons responsible for any failure to meet organizational goals and objectives (i.e., "fix blame"). In contrast, the control systems established in Japanese firms relied heavily on group responsibility for group performance and "saving face" rather than "fixing blame" was important to maintenance of harmony and respect for the Japanese. As part of this approach, Japanese companies relied heavily on group improvement processes such as quality control circles, a practice that was rarely seen in the United States until the late 1980s when US companies began to seriously consider whether Japanese management practices might work in the United States. Weihrich believed that China lied somewhere in between the United States and Japan with respect to control. The group leader, the senior manager, was expected to exercise control over the group and while the group assumed responsibility for pursuing and achieving group goals and objectives there was a stronger level of

---

[66] Culpan, R., and O. Kucukemiroglu. 1993. "A Comparison of US and Japanese Management Styles and Unit Effectiveness." *Management International Review* 33, pp. 27–42. (citing Pascale, R.T. 1978. "Communications and Decision-making: Cross-Cultural Comparisons." *Administrative Science Quarterly* 23, pp. 91–110).

[67] Id.

individual responsibility for Chinese workers than for Japanese workers. Nonetheless, as in Japan, "saving face" was important in China. Strategies such as quality control circles enjoyed limited popularity in China.

Culpan and Kucukemiroglu assessed differences between US and Japanese managers with respect to "control mechanisms," which they defined to include "comparison of standards with outcomes" and the processes that managers used to check on the conduct of operational activities to determine whether the results achieved by subordinates in carrying out those activities meet the performance goals and standards established by the organization.[68] The variables relevant to assessing control mechanisms are similar in many respects to those used in evaluating supervisory style. One approach to control is to implement "close supervision" procedures that feature extensive involvement of managers in the activities of their subordinates and extensive interim check of performance against the goals set for the activities. One the other hand, managers may be willing to accept "democratic supervision" and afford their subordinates more freedom to schedule their own activities and rely on the unit to develop and follow the specific processes needed to achieve its goals rather than imposing limits and restrictions on the process of obtaining the desired final outcomes. In other words, emphasis is placed on "production" as a goal rather than focusing too much on the details of how the production process should work.

It is generally accepted that control processes that achieve uniformity and support coordination within the organization are important contributors to attaining of organizational goals and overall organizational effectiveness. It is also well known that decisions regarding control mechanisms impact the elements of the organizational design of the firm, particularly the organizational structure: tight control generally leads to centralization and tall hierarchical structures. Culpan and Kucukemiroglu noted that Ouchi had reported that distinctions could be made between US and Japanese managerial practices with respect to control, with US managers preferring "explicit" control based on setting specific and measurable performance targets while Japanese managers relied on "implicit" control

---

[68] Id.

built on "philosophy of management governing organizational and individual behavior."[69]

Decision Making

Culpan and Kucukemiroglu defined "decision making" as "the process in which decisions are made within the unit and the extent to which employees contribute to or participate to managerial decisions."[70] Admittedly, there is some overlap between this dimension and the analysis of "participation" in the context of identifying supervisory styles. Some of the elements that are analyzed in evaluating decision-making processes include the degree to which the supervisor solicits inputs and opinions from subordinates, the use of processes that include subordinate participation in decision making and building a consensus among subordinates for the chosen strategies, the level of permitted individual decision-making by subordinates, and the processes used to identify and attempt improvements in processes and innovative methods and products. Suggested measures of how the decision-making process works in reality include the number of suggestions made by subordinates and the number of projects that were launched in spite of the lack of support and enthusiasm from subordinates.[71] Culpan and Kucukemiroglu surveyed the literature and noted that different approaches to decision making could be found across organizations and countries including distinctions between long- and short-range orientations,[72] results versus processes, and authoritarian versus democratic approaches.[73] Culpan and Kucukemiroglu were particularly interested in Japanese management styles and thus noted the great interest in the "ringi" system, which was the consensus-oriented process

---

[69] Id. (citing Ouchi, W. 1981. *Theory Z—How American Business Can Meet the Japanese Challenge.* Reading, MA: Addison-Wesley).

[70] Culpan, R., and O. Kucukemiroglu. 1993. "A Comparison of US and Japanese Management Styles and Unit Effectiveness." *Management International Review* 33, pp. 27–42.

[71] Id.

[72] Ouchi, W. 1981. *Theory Z—How American Business Can Meet the Japanese Challenge.* Reading, MA: Addison-Wesley.

[73] Likert, R. 1961. *New Patterns of Management.* New York, NY: McGraw-Hill.

for making decisions, which was frequently used in Japan and often suggested as a candidate for transfer to American firms.[74]

Adler also analyzed the organizational decision-making processes by identifying and examining what she considered to be the five basic steps of decision making—problem recognition, information search, construction of alternative solutions, selection among the alternative solutions (i.e., "decision"), and implementation of decisions—and, in each case, he concluded that there were significant differences in the way that people from different cultures approach each of them.[75] With regard to problem recognition a distinction could be made between cultures such as the United States in which managers are "problem solvers" and cultures such as those emanating from East Asia in which managers tend to be "problem accepters." Problem solvers have a high level of confidence in their ability to identify problems and find solutions through their own efforts while problem accepters react more passively and tend to accept difficulties without challenge as simply being "God's will." Adler argued that problem solvers identified problems long before problem accepters were willing to admit that a problem existed. With regard to information search, Adler argued that persons from Western cultures were more deductive and used all five of their senses to gather information needed to make a decision while persons from Asia cultures acted more on their intuition and used ideas from their past to guide their efforts to gather information. With regard to construction of alternatives, Western cultures, which tend to be more future-oriented than Asian cultures, were more likely to create new alternatives (solutions) for problems than their colleagues from Asian cultures that relied heavily on historical precedents for guidance.

---

[74] See, e.g., Pascale, R.T. 1978. "Communications and Decision-making: Cross-cultural Comparisons." *Administrative Science Quarterly* 23, pp. 91–110; Rohlen, T. 1974. *For Harmony and Strength*. Berkeley, CA: University of California Press; and Vogel, E. 1979. *Japan as Number One: Lessons for America*. Cambridge, MA: Harvard University Press.

[75] Adler, N. 1991. *International Dimensions of Organizational Behavior*, 14–178, 2nd ed. Boston, MA: PWS-Kent Publishing Co.

Nigam and Su analyzed decision making by assessing the level of power delegation in the societal management culture, with a particular focus on India.[76] They noted that the caste system and impact of Hinduism had both contributed to a high power distance in India and this had led to adoption of a hierarchical model in which authority was more centralized and decision making is "top-down."[77] Power is considered to be an important managerial motivation in India and, in fact, Nigam and Su noted that "the behavior of managers in a normal Indian firm may be described as a combination of collectivism on the outside and individualism on the inside." As a result, Indian managers are loath to delegating power and authority. Nigam and Su contrasted the situation in India to "developed cultures" where "decentralized power provides more motivation to employees"[78] and cited studies that showed that employee participation in decision making and strategic planning processes had a positive impact on employee performance, motivation and confidence.[79]

Motivation

While "motivation" is not one of the managerial functions typically identified as among the most important, there is ample evidence that the most effective managers are actively engaged in improving employee performance and motivating employees by understanding and attempt to meet

---

[76] R. Nigam and Z. Su, "Management in Emerging versus Developed Countries: A Comparative Study from an Indian Perspective," *Journal of CENTRUM Cathedra*, 4, no. 1, pp. 121–33.

[77] Id. at 126.

[78] Id. at 126 (citing Chatterjee, S. 2007. "Bridging the Gap between Potential and Performance: The Challenges of Indian Management." In *Asian Management in Transition: Emerging Themes*, eds. S. Chatterjee and A. Nankervis, 83. London: Palgrave Macmillan).

[79] Wagner, J. 1994. "Participation's Effect on Performance and Satisfaction: A Reconsideration of Research Evidence." *Academy of Management Review* 19, pp. 312–31; Kim, S. 2002. "Participative Management and Job Satisfaction: Lessons for Management Leadership." *Public Administration Review* 62, no. 2, pp. 231–41.

their needs and expectations.[80] Motivation is one of the key challenges of human resources management and researchers have observed that while motivational practices do not directly influence organizational performance, they do influence human capital, which, in turn, does have a major impact on organizational performance.[81] There are a number of different human resources tools and practices that can be categorized as elements of "motivation" including compensation, promotion and rewards, performance appraisals, training and development, and career planning.

Adler examined a number of the well-known motivation theories that had originated in the United States including theories proposed by Maslow, McClelland, Herzberg, and Vroom.[82] Adler argued that security is more important than self-actualization as a motivating factor in

[80] Cameron, K.S., and D. Whetten. 1983. "A Model for Teaching Management Skills." *Organizational Behavior Teaching Journal* 8, no. 2, pp. 21–27.

[81] Nigam, R., and Z. Su. 2011. "Management in Emerging versus Developed Countries: A Comparative Study from an Indian Perspective." *Journal of CENTRUM Cathedra* 4, no. 1, pp. 121–33, 125. (citing Dimba, B., P. K'Obonyo, and R. Kiraka. 2008. *The Effect of Strategic Human Resource Management Practices on Organizational Performance of Manufacturing Multinational Companies in Kenya: The Mediating Role of Employee Motivation*. Strathmore University, Faculty of Commerce). With respect to the relationship between human resources activities and motivating employees, see also Boudreau, J. 1998. "Strategic Human Resource Management Measures: Key Linkages and the People Vantage Model." Working Paper No. 28. Cornell University, Center for Advanced Human Resource Studies; Nadler, D., and E. Lawler III. 1977. "Motivation: A Diagnostic Approach." In *Perspectives on Behavior in Organizations*, eds. J. Hackman, E. Lawler III and L. Porter, 26–38, New York, NY: McGraw-Hill; and Park, H., H. Mitsuhashi, C. Fey and I. Bjorkman, "The Effect of Human Resource Management Practices on Japanese MNC Subsidiary Performance—A Partial Mediating Model." Working Paper No. 3, St Petersburg, Sweden: Stockholm School of Economics.

[82] Adler, N. 1991. *International Dimensions of Organizational Behavior*, 2nd ed. Boston, MA: PWS-Kent Publishing Co, pp. 14–178. Adler examined many of the same US-based theories that Hofstede cited during his discussion of the applicability of American motivational theories to organizations rooted in different societal cultures in Hofstede, G. 1980. "Motivation, Leadership and Organization: Do American Theories Apply Abroad." *Organization Dynamics* 9, no. 1, pp. 42–63.

countries like China and Japan that have a higher level of uncertainty avoidance. On the other hand, in countries where there is a high need for achievement or that have a higher score on the masculinity dimension, people are more likely to be driven to produce and comfortable with taking on more risk as opposed to worrying about avoiding uncertainty. Adler pointed out that while there was a certain logical validity to Vroom's well-known "expectancy theory," which is based on the proposition that when firms suitably reward their employees those employees will be more likely to conduct themselves in ways that ensure that they will receive those rewards; as a practical matter, cultural factors will play an important part in determining whether a specific type of reward system will have the desired motivational effect.[83] In addition, there are differences between cultures with regard to the amount of control that persons believe that they have over their environment and these differences should also be taken into account when designing a reward system. For example, managers and employees in the United States tend to have a stronger belief that they can control the rewards they receive from their work through the amount of effort that they spend on their jobs. In that situation, a reward system based on productivity may be appropriate and effective. On the other hand, however, a productivity-based reward system may not have the desired impact with managers and employees from Hong Kong who tend to see the likelihood of their success in work activities as a combination of their own efforts and luck ("joss"). Japan offered still another dimension with respect to motivation given that harmony with and among work colleagues is so important that employees may be uninterested in participating in a reward system that might result in him or her gaining an advantage (e.g., a promotion) that causes separation from those colleagues.

It is generally agreed that compensation is one of the most important methods for motivating employees and may be directed toward individual goals and/or organizational objectives. Compensation packages

---

[83] See Vroom, V. 1964. *Work and Motivation*. New York, NY: Wiley. The expectancy Theory makes no assumption regarding the preferred form of reward and thus rewards may take a number of different forms based on the societal culture (i.e., money, promotion, recognition etc.).

include both monetary and nonmonetary benefits and researchers such as Minbaeva have suggested that companies adopt strategically planned compensation systems that include the base salary, flexible pay, and benefits allocated in a selective fashion in order to better motivate employees lead them toward effective performance.[84] Many studies have provided support for the notion that societal culture plays a big role in the motivational impact of the various compensation and reward tools. For example, in some cultures money is a very strong motivating factor[85] while in other countries money was not as important as instant and personal recognition, status, a pleasurable job experience, and programs that encouraged personal well-being (e.g., maternity leaves, sabbaticals, subsidies for medical care, and housing and educational programs).[86] In general, the research seems to indicate that money-based compensation elements—basic salary, merit pay, bonuses, and profit sharing—tend to have a greater impact in more individualistic societies[87] while employees in collectivist societies prefer, and have come to expect, the support associated with a long-term

---

[84] Minbaeva, D.B. 2008. "HRM Practices Affecting Extrinsic and Intrinsic Motivation of Knowledge Receivers and Their Effect on intra-MNC Knowledge Transfer." *International Business Review* 17, no. 6, pp. 703–13 (cited in Nigam, R., and Z. Su. 2011. "Management in Emerging versus Developed Countries: A Comparative Study from an Indian Perspective." *Journal of CENTRUM Cathedra* 4, no 1, pp. 121–33, 126).

[85] Bock, G., R. Zmud, Y. Kim, and J. Lee. 2005. "Behavioral Intention Formation in Knowledge Sharing: Examining the Roles of Extrinsic Motivators, Social-Psychological Forces and Organizational Climate." *MIS Quarterly* 29, no. 1, pp. 87–112.

[86] Nelson, B. 1996. *1001 Ways to Reward Employees*. New York, NY: Workman; J. Lang, "Human Resources in India: Retaining and Motivating Staff in a Lufthansa Subsidiary." *Compensation Benefits Review* 40, pp. 56–62; Aycan, Z. 2005. "The Interplay between Cultural and Institutional/Structural Contingencies in Human Resource Management Practices." *International Journal of Human Resource Management* 16, no. 7, pp. 1083–119; and Chatterjee, S. 2007. "Human Resource Management in India: 'Where from' and 'Where to?'" *Research and Practice in Human Resource Management* 15, no. 2, pp. 92–103.

[87] Chiu, R., V. Luk, and T. Tang. 2002. "Retaining and Motivating Employees: Compensation Preferences in Hong Kong and China." *Personnel Review* 31, no. 4, pp. 402–31.

relationship with their employer that includes extensive involvement by employers in the personal lives and well-being of members of their workforces.

Nigam and Su also observed that "collectivist and individualist cultures also give rise to different kinds of reward schemes" and that "special recognition for one employee may not be an effective idea in collective culture."[88] Acknowledging that rewards based on individual performance, such as bonuses and stock options, are good motivators in individualists cultures and generally enhance firm performance, Nigam and Su suggested that a different approach was appropriate for firms in collectivist cultures. In India, for example, distribution of rewards is based on a philosophy of equality and managers and workers have generally been willing to accept that raises and promotions would be based on loyalty and seniority as part of the overall bargain of lifetime employment.[89] This approach to determination and distribution of rewards tends to encourage cooperation rather than competition among workers and also means that relatively little attention is paid to formal objective appraisal systems that are used in individualistic countries to measure performance in order to determine rewards and establish career paths and training objectives for employees.[90]

Muczyk and Holt also emphasized the importance of taking regional cultural characteristics into account when designing and administering performance management and reward programs.[91] They noted, for

[88] Nigam, R., and Z. Su. 2011. "Management in Emerging versus Developed Countries: A Comparative Study from an Indian Perspective." *Journal of CENTRUM Cathedra* 4, no. 1, pp. 121–33, 126.

[89] Ramamoorthy, N., A. Gupta, R. Sardessai, and P. Flood. 2005. "Individualism / Collectivism and Attitudes Towards Human Resource Systems: A Comparative Study of American, Irish and Indian MBA Students." *International Journal of Human Resource Management* 16, no. 5, pp. 852–69.

[90] Nigam, R., and Z. Su. 2011. "Management in Emerging versus Developed Countries: A Comparative Study from an Indian Perspective." *Journal of CENTRUM Cathedra* 4, no. 1, pp. 121–33, 127.

[91] Muczyk, J.P., and D.T. Holt. May 2008. "Toward a Cultural Contingency Model of Leadership." *Journal of Leadership & Organizational Studies* 14, no. 4, pp. 277–86, 283–84. (citing Nadler, N. 2002. *International Dimensions of Organizational Behavior*, 4th ed. Cincinnati, OH: Southwestern).

example, that "leaders in the Middle East would be best served if rewards were linked to measures of group or organizational performance" but that "[i]n Europe, leaders would want to link rewards to individual outcomes rather than to organizational outcomes." Japan presented an interesting special case in their minds since they found that rewards and incentives did not appear to be that important to employees of Japanese organizations and that they tend to take the required actions not to be "rewarded" but simply because it was the right thing to do.

In Mexico it can be problematic to attempt to motivate Mexican workers using rewards systems that are based on their own actions and performance since many Mexican workers believe that events in their lives are the result of forces beyond their control. Work is often seen primarily as the means for providing for the needs of the worker and his or her family rather than as a path for pursuit of individual achievement. Placed in the framework of Maslow's hierarchy of needs, most Mexican workers are most concerned with their current survival and livelihood rather than higher order needs such as self-actualization, achievement, and status. This is not surprising given the difficult economic conditions in Mexico and relatively low standard of living and dictates that compensation systems for many workers be geared toward short-term incentives and goals, such as meeting daily production quotas and satisfying monthly requirements for regular daily attendance.[92] Use of variable compensation programs may also be problematic in Mexico because they can create "social distance among employees" and as a rule Mexican employees, even though they are often struggling to get by, prefer a congenial work environment as opposed to the chance to make more money in a compensation program that set employees up as competitors of one another.[93] Variable compensation programs are also inconsistent with the high uncertainty avoidance in Mexico, which leads employees to dislike unstable and ambiguous situations such as not knowing how much they will be paid and when payment will be received.

---

[92] Resource for Business Management, "Comparative Motivation in Mexico: Management in Focus." https://coursehero.com/file/p7vjbq5q/Comparative-Management-in-Focus-Motivation-in-Mexico-see-slide-11-11-11-12-To/ (accessed December 31, 2018).

[93] Id.

While economic conditions in Mexico dictate that cash compensation, generally based on simple short-term payment systems, is the primary motivational factor for Mexican workers, companies often provide additional benefits such as recreational facilities, on-site health care facilities for workers and their families, free meals, and, in some instances, small loans to help workers and their families get through unforeseen emergencies. These benefits are seen as part of the paternalistic role that Mexican firms play with respect to their workers and help to build a sense of family within the firm. The viability of performance-based compensation arrangements in Mexico is undermined by legal requirements that workers be paid Christmas bonuses regardless of productivity.[94]

Performance appraisal is slowly but surely becoming an important part of human resources management as companies realize that appraisal systems can be a useful tool in improving overall company performance by motivating well-performing employees and creating strategies for improving the skills of laggards. There are, however, a number of challenges associated with performance appraisal including selecting the methods used to evaluate performance and deliver the results to employees. In addition, consideration must be given to cultural context and Nigam and Su observed that researchers have found that "explaining, formal, objective and individual appraisal methods are more accepted in individualist cultures like North America, which encourage goal achievement; on the other hand, in collectivist cultures like India use of informal, subjective appraisal is more popular."[95] In fact, several researchers have noted that performance appraisal methods in India are crude or nonexistent and when appraisals are carried out, they are limited only to a certain level of employees.[96]

---

[94] Id.

[95] Nigam, R., and S. Zhang. 2011. "Management in Emerging versus Developed Countries: A Comparative Study from an Indian Perspective." *Journal of CENTRUM Cathedra* 4, no.1, pp. 121–33, 127 (citing Stone, D.L., E. Stone-Romero, and K. Lukaszewski. 2007. "The Impact of Cultural Values on The Acceptance and Effectiveness of Human Resource Management Policies and Practices." *Human Resource Management Review* 17, no. 2, pp. 152–65).

[96] Chatterjee, S.R. 2007. "Human Resource Management in India: 'Where from' and 'Where to?'" *Research and Practice in Human Resource Management* 15, no. 2,

Nigam and Su defined training and development "as a course of action for developing work-related skills and awareness in employees with the intention of making the firm's performance more effective."[97] Training and development contributes to firm performance by improving the skills and motivation of employees. In addition, training and development can be used to bolster control and coordination within large organizations with widely dispersed business units. It has been argued that training and development is most effective when it is closely aligned with the goals of the firm and training and development activities should focus on the skills needed to achieve those goals. Researchers such as Chatterjee and Aycan have observed that training and development has not been effective in developing the skills and values of employees in developing countries such as India and that training and development in collectivist countries such as India is often used to increase loyalty to the company as opposed to improving personal skills.[98] Another issue in developing countries is that selection to participating in training programs is based not on the requirements of the company but on favoritism (i.e., employees with good relationships with their superiors are more likely to be chosen for training programs).

pp. 92–103; Mendonca, M., and R. Kanungo. 1990 "Performance Management in Developing Countries." In *Management in Developing Countries*, eds. R. Kanungo and A. Jaeger, 223–251. London, UK: Routledge.; Baruch, Y., and P. Budhwar. 2008. "A Comparative Study for Career Practices for Management Staff in India and Britain." *International Business Review* 15, no. 1, pp. 84–101; and Rao, A. 2007. "Effectiveness of Performance Management Systems: An Empirical Study in Indian Companies." *The International Journal of Human Resource Management* 18, no. 10, pp. 1812–40.

[97] Nigam, R., and Zhang, Su. 2011. "Management in Emerging versus Developed Countries: A Comparative Study from an Indian Perspective." *Journal of CENTRUM Cathedra* 4, no. 1, pp. 121–133, 127.

[98] Aycan, Z. 2005. "The Interplay between Cultural and Institutional/Structural Contingencies in Human Resource Management Practices." *International Journal of Human Resource Management* 16, no. 7, pp. 1083–119; and Chatterjee, S.R. 2007. "Human Resource Management in India: 'Where from' and 'Where to?'" *Research and Practice in Human Resource Management* 15, no. 2, pp. 92–103.

CHAPTER 3

National Business Cultures

Introduction

When comparative management studies first emerged as a recognized discipline and body of research the implicit assumption often was that there were universal management styles and practices that could and should be transferred anywhere in the world. Inevitably these styles and practices were based upon US experiences since the United States played a dominant role in global trade and most of the research and commentary on the subject came from the United States. However, as time has gone by it has become clear that a manager from one country cannot assume that he or she will be able to seamlessly transfer and embed management styles, practices, processes, and expectations from his or her country into another country and that his or her effectiveness as a manager will depend on developing a profile of the national societal culture that identified differences, which must be taken into account in acting as a manager.

In general, the national societal culture includes the various norms, behaviors, beliefs, and customs that can be found among the people of a particular country. A wide range of dimensions have been suggested for use as the basis for identifying and comparing differences between societal cultures in various countries that might eventually influence the effectiveness of managerial behaviors and the expectations of subordinates regarding the actions taken by their superiors. Overlapping dimensions used by Hofstede and the GLOBE researchers included power distance, uncertainty avoidance, institutional collectivism versus individualism, and gender differentiation (i.e., the masculinity–femininity pole), and the GLOBE researchers also suggested and analyzed four additional dimensions: assertiveness, future orientation, performance orientation, and humane orientation. Many of the dimensions identified by Trompenaars were similar to those used by Hofstede and the GLOBE researchers;

however, he added several other potential variables including obligation, emotional orientation, privacy, and the source of power and status.

Regardless of which dimensions are used to identify and analyze cultural differences between countries, it is agreed that the differences are a function of deeply rooted values that permeate all aspects of life in the country including the workplace and the ways in which business relationships are formed and managed. For managers, awareness of the national business culture is essential to knowing what subordinates expect of their organizational leaders and developing a style and set of behaviors that will be effective in satisfying subordinates and motivating them to perform their jobs in a way that achieves the goals and objectives of the business. National business cultures include not only the values and norms that form the societal culture but also include the consensus among the population regarding the role of economic and political institutions that impact commerce.

An understanding of the applicable national business culture should be coupled with an awareness of the dominant traits and characteristics of customary management styles and practices. While many have argued that the increasing rate of globalization in the business arena is causing convergence among management styles that is overriding cultural differences, researchers continue to explore the characteristics of specific national management styles.[1] Some studies focus specifically on one country, a process referred to by anthropologists as ethnography and which includes in-depth analysis and description of the customary social behaviors of a single identifiable group of people using techniques such as participant observation; however, a good deal of what appears in more recent assessments of national management styles is based on the practice of ethnology, which is the comparative study of two or more cultures that looks at a narrower set of data related to a particular topic and seeks to compare and contrast the various cultures.

There are several different models of management style that may be used for descriptive and comparative purposes. One method for modeling

---

[1] Information on management styles and practices in various countries is available in the Regional and Countries Studies materials prepared and distributed by the Sustainable Entrepreneurship Project (www.seproject.org).

a manager's style and practices focuses on a small set of specific characteristics and activities such as supervisory style, decision making style and processes, communication patterns, control mechanisms, management of interdepartmental relationships, and, finally, the strength of paternalistic orientation when interacting with subordinates.[2] Another method of describing "management styles," which may be particularly useful when studying developing countries is the model created by Khandwalla after studying 90 organizations in India, research that caused him to recognize and describe ten categories of management styles: conservative, entrepreneurial, professional, bureaucratic, organic, authoritarian, participative, intuitive, familial, and altruistic.[3]

National Business Cultures

Managers in every country must act within the boundaries of various institutions and values that, taken together, form what can usefully be referred to as the "national business culture" for that country. A unique national business culture arises due to differences in major social institutions, differences in approaches to economic organization, and ownership and control of resources (e.g., "capitalism" versus "socialism") and, of course, variations between countries with respect to the values underlying their societal cultures and the political systems that have been adapted to govern the citizens and promulgate and enforce the laws that regulate activities within the country. National business culture is also impacted by history, including colonial occupation, religion, the availability of capital, the availability of natural resources, human capital, technology, demographic factors, and communications with other societies. All in all, national business culture is heavily influenced by a wide array of behavioral and institutional elements that also impact the way in which managers act and the effectiveness of those actions in furthering the achievement

[2] Culpan, R., and O. Kucukemiroglu. 1993. "A Comparison of US and Japanese Management Styles and Unit Effectiveness." *Management International Review*, 33–27.

[3] Khandwalla, P.N. 1995. "Effectiveness Management Styles: An Indian Study." *Journal of Euro-Asian Management* 1, no. 1, pp. 43–46, 39.

of organizational goals.[4] The sections that follow provide an overview of American, European, and Asian business cultures.

American Business Culture

Profiles of American culture have emphasized characteristics such as goal and achievement orientation, desire, and passion for freedom, self-reliance, work orientation, and competitiveness. A profile of American culture developed by Linowes was built around three fundamental characteristics: action, freedom, and equality.[5] Specific attitudes and behaviors associated with each of these characteristics included the following:

- Action: Man controlling nature, risk-taking, bold initiative, spontaneity, improvisation, outspokenness, critical thinking, logical reasoning, clarity and frankness, decisiveness
- Freedom: Individuality, individual independence, legal safeguards, righteous indignation, being heard, chaotic anarchy, proving oneself
- Equality: Level-playing field, industrial competition, track record, rewarding performance, specialists, opportunities, autonomy, ambiguous/informal ranking, racial and gender equality

As such, it is not surprising that American business culture has long exemplified, and glorified, a sort of "rugged individualism" that has

---

[4] Glunk et al. noted that "[[i]n order to provide a realistic picture of a national management style, one has to consider behavioral as well as institutional aspects of the business system". Glunk, U., C. Wilderom, and R. Ogilvie. 1996. "Finding the Key to German-Style Management." *International Studies of Management and Organization* 26, no. 3, pp. 93–108, 93 (citing Whitley, R. 1992. *European Business Systems*. London: Sage Publications; and Whitley, R. 1994. "Dominant Forms of Economic Organization in Market Economies." *Organization Studies* 15, no. 2, pp. 153–82).

[5] Linowes, R.G. November 1993. "The Japanese Manager's Traumatic Entry into the United States: Understanding the American–Japanese Cultural Divide." *The Academy of Management Executive* 7, no. 4, p. 24.

evidenced itself in what are perceived as relatively high levels of tension and confrontation within and between companies and between the business community on the one hand and legislative and regulatory bodies on the other hand. There has been, in general, a marked level of distrust between business and government in the United States and this has often led to extensive attempts to regulate the activities of corporations in a number of areas including antitrust, consumer protection, securities regulation, and, most recently, corporate governance. All this contrasts markedly with the close business–government relations in other parts of the world such as Europe and Asia, which have often been criticized by US policy makers and endlessly debated in countless international forums on global trading matters.[6]

Interestingly, while "rugged individualism" is definitely part of the overall business environment in the United States, the traditional model for designing the organization structure of American businesses has been quite formalistic and relies heavily on hierarchical structure, standards, and systems and focused specialization among workers. In what almost seems to be a concerted effort to regulate "individualism" in the workplace, US companies have generally been more likely than their counterparts in foreign countries to create formal and defined organizational structures, prepare detailed written job descriptions, promulgate and monitor quantifiable performance standards, and issue lengthy policies and manuals covering all aspects of operational activities carried out within the company. American public companies, as well as privately held emerging companies with professional investors such as venture capitalists, have also emphasized short-term financial performance as the key measure of how their strategies and structures are working. This

---

[6] The discussion of American business culture in this section is adapted from Humes, S. 1993. *Managing the Multinational: Confronting the Global-Local Dilemma*, 113–16. Prentice Hall International (UK) Ltd., Hemel Hempstead, Hertfordshire UK. For discussion of business-government relations in the United States, see R. Porter, Government-Business Relations in the United States, Paper for Transatlantic Perspectives on US-EU Economic Relations: Convergence, Conflict and Cooperation at Harvard University John F. Kennedy School of Government (April 8, 2002).

preoccupation with "making the numbers" on a monthly, quarterly, and annual basis, and demonstrating continuous improvements in growth and profitability, has been fostered by several other American institutional factors—the demands of US financial markets and investors for quick returns and impatience with investment projects that have long "payout" periods and the greater emphasis that has traditionally been placed on quantitative analysis in US business schools as they train the future managers of US companies.

One specific characteristic of American business that has an important impact on organizational structure is the historical emphasis on specialization. As noted earlier, US companies have typically relied heavily on specific job descriptions and settling well-defined responsibilities for managers and employees at all levels within the company. This approach parallels the development of education, training, and certification in the United States and one can easily recognize the importance and prevalence of professional and technical specialties and specialized educational programs in accounting, finance, law, engineering, and the sciences that are accompanied by extensive postgraduate networking that reinforce the specialty connections. Many American managers began their careers as specialists, as opposed to "general management," and usually spend their formative years in the corporate world working in fairly narrow functional areas and responsibilities. In general, American companies looking to bring on new recruits will populate their offices by reference to specialist needs as opposed to selecting persons who may not have the currently required background yet is more likely to emerge as a leader in the future. The focus on specialization also means that US companies are usually comfortable with recruiting and hiring from outside the current worker population if necessary to access particular specialist skills.

American businesses are also well known for their emphasis and fascination with the concept of "professional management." As evidenced by the respect afforded graduate management training, the "MBA" in particular, US companies have generally accepted the idea that corporations and other for-profit and not-for-profit organizations can be effectively managed through the application of generic concepts and techniques. This belief has fostered the development of a whole cottage industry of constantly changing management techniques that are delivered and disseminated by countless management consultants and "gurus." Through the magical use of mass-marketing techniques American managers have been bombarded with a continuous stream of new tools and ideas to fulfill their responsibilities including calls for commitment to vague and general concepts such as "excellence," "quality," "innovation," "customer satisfaction," and "culture." In fact, much of the discussion regarding organizational structure and design has been updated to incorporate buzzwords such as "value chains," "strategic business units," "diversification," and "portfolio management." While some of this information has been interesting, topical, and innovative, there are numerous examples of "new theories" that are simply recycled versions of earlier ideas. Moreover, the American bias toward short-term results often leads to poorly thought out decisions to quickly embrace a new "fad" without carefully analyzing the underlying foundations and determining whether it is best suited to the activities and culture of the specific organization. It is not surprising that "one-minute managing" found a welcome audience among managers of US companies. It should be noted that, in general, managers outside the United States view these new management theories and ideas as interesting background reading and something to ponder as opposed to a specific blueprint that needs to be implemented immediately.

For all of the generalizations made earlier about American businesses, it is only fair to note that one can still find tremendous diversity with respect to the cultures that have been adopted in successful US corporations. Certainly there are numerous examples of corporations that have interpreted "rugged individualism" to mean that managers and other employees must continuously compete internally for resources and assignments and that the spoils will go only to those that prove to be the "fittest." On the other hand, confrontation and internal competition is tempered in many companies by attempts to cultivate a sense of "family" and belonging through training and other human resources programs designed to assist and support managers and employees in their efforts to improve and contribute to the company on a long-term basis. Some companies measure performance, and distribute rewards, strictly "by the numbers," while other make a great effort to identify and reward more intangible contributions such as "creativity" and "innovation." Dominant management styles also vary—"hierarchical" at one end to "participative" at the other end—and studies of organizational culture within emerging companies have noted the significant role that founders play in defining and establishing a management culture for their firms that remains in place long after the founders have been replaced by professional managers who were not involved in the initial launch of the company. Even more challenging is the attempt by many larger organizations with diverse business lines to allow for cultures and management approaches to vary from division to division as necessary to achieve strategic objectives (i.e., "intrapreneuring").

The dramatic and well-publicized successes and failures among companies in Silicon Valley have captured the interest of legions of researchers and consultants interested in defining and understanding the management styles deployed in those companies. In the 1980s, Rogers and Larsen found that the primary reason for the failure of high-technology companies in Silicon Valley was poor management, as opposed to lack of capital, technical difficulties with products, or poor human resources. In turn, the successful firms were those in which senior management delegated authority and closely monitored all products and systems.[7]

Many books and articles have traced the development of the "Silicon Valley approach" to management and the stories generally begin back in the 1940s and 1950s with iconic firms such as Varian Associates and Hewlett Packard ("HP"). Important managerial characteristics of these companies included the removal of restrictions on pursuit of new ideas and innovations; employee participation in the company's successes through the use of stock options, a strategy intended to foster cooperation and enthusiasm throughout the workforce; emphasis on teamwork; and the ability to manage rapid change. A famous story, often retold, about the beginnings of Silicon Valley focuses on the decision in 1957 of eight employees of Shockley Labs to abandon the firm led by William Shockley, a Nobel Prize-winning co-inventor of the transistor, to form Fairchild Semiconductor to escape Shockley's intense micromanagement and forge their own company based on "open communications, laissez-faire management styles, flat organizational structures, and generous distributions

[7] Rogers, E.M., and J.K Larsen. 1984. *Silicon Valley: Fever-Growth of High Technology Culture*. Basic Books (AZ).

of stock options."[8] Bernshteyn argued for the proposition that successful Silicon Valley firms operated under a nontraditional management style that fostered growth, creativity, innovation, and employee retention and relied on a "bottom-up" approach that began with finding and hiring the brightest and most nimble managers and employees, finding the right place in the organizational structure to maximize their strengths, and empowering those employees by avoiding excessive direction and rulemaking from the top.[9]

HP is often held out as the premier example of the original Silicon Valley management style and the management philosophy articulated by the founders of HP, Bill Hewlett and David Packard, became known as the "HP Way" and included respect and trust for the individual, hiring the best people and matching them to the right job; contribution to the customer and the community, integrity, teamwork, innovation, and continuous learning with the help of customer feedback.[10] Carly Fiorina revised and updated the HP Way as the "Rules of the Garage" in 1999 and admonished HP employees to believe they could change the world; work quickly, keep their tools unlocked, and work whenever; know when to work alone and when to work together; share tools and ideas and trust their colleagues; set aside politics and bureaucracy; accept that it is the customer that defines a job well done; acknowledge that radical ideas are not bad ideas; invent different ways of working; make a contribution every day; and believe that together HP employees could do anything.

While the Silicon Valley management style has been widely praised, and attempts to emulate it have proliferated around the world, some have expressed concerns about some of the consequences of focusing too much on managing change through flexibility and embracing "lean and mean" resources management strategies. Pfeffer, for example, began with the premise that the model of Silicon Valley management that had emerged

---

[8] Berlin, L. September 2, 2005. "How the Valley Start-Up was Invented: William Shockley Drove His Team Nuts." *San Jose Mercury News* http://leslieberlinauthor. com/wp-content/uploads/2011/05/HowtheValleyStart-UpwasInvented.pdf

[9] Travios, D. June 15, 2012. "The Secret Sauce of Silicon Valley." *Forbes.*

[10] Towers, S. 2002. "The Silicon Valley Management Style." http://itstime.com/apr2002.htm

by the early 2000s was based on four basic ideas: a "free agent" model of employment that demanded that employees look out for themselves and be prepared and willing to move on—change jobs—at a moment's notice; extensive reliance on teams of outside contractors that could be expanded or reduced quickly and efficiently; use of stock options as an important element of compensation; and the belief that value to the organization was measured by the number of hours worked (i.e., working long hours was the norm).[11] He noted that companies built on these principles would presumably be well positioned to pivot quickly as their environments shifted; however, he suggested that the free agent mentality created excessively high turnover that was actually quite costly to companies in terms of having to recruit and train new staff, manage and minimize disruption to relationships with customers and other strategic partners, and worry about whether former employees were using their ideas in new jobs with competitors. Pfeffer also questioned whether outsourcing was conducive to building a sustained competitive advantage since a large portion of the knowledge generated during outsourcing arrangements resided outside of the company.

European Business Culture

For all the talk and action associated with integration of European economic activities, it remains likely that the management cultures of European companies will continue to hark back to their specific national roots.[12] As such, when observing and defining the management culture for a particular European company, it is essential to identify and understand the impact of environmental factors such as language, history and tradition, educational systems, and social class systems in its home

---

[11] Pfeffer, J. Spring 2001. "What's Wrong With Management Practices in Silicon Valley? A Lot." *Sloan Management Review*, http://sloanreview.mit.edu/article/whats-wrong-with-management-practices-in-silicon-valley-a-lot/

[12] The discussion of European business culture in this section is adapted from Humes, S. 1993. *Managing the Multinational: Confronting the Global-Local Dilemma*, 118–21. Prentice Hall International (UK) Ltd. Hemel Hempstead, Hertfordshire UK.

country regardless of how the geographic reach of its operational activities may have expanded into other countries and regions. In fact, within the membership of the European Union one can probably identify a number of different "country clusters" of similar business cultures including Anglo (e.g., United Kingdom), Germanic (e.g., Germany, Austria, and Switzerland), Latin European (e.g., France, Italy, and Spain), Nordic (e.g., Denmark, Finland, Norway, and Sweden) and Near Eastern (e.g., Greece and Turkey)[13]; however, while these categories do have some utility any attempt to derive universal rules and expectations regarding managerial practices and employee attitudes should be undertaken with caution.

There is some degree of truth to generalizations made about British, French, German, and Italian managers and the companies that they oversee. For example, it has been said that the characteristics of management culture in the UK include a stress on common sense, adaptability, and resourceful pragmatism along with class and club-consciousness. Traditionally, UK companies had little interest in formal business training for their managers and opted for "gentlemen amateurs" with either no degree or a liberal arts degree as their foundation for taking on a management role. However, beginning in the early 1990s accounting began to emerge as a preferred specialist background in the UK and there was also a definite movement toward management training in universities and colleges. Explanations of German management culture include an emphasis on order, discipline, and efficiency and a respect for professional expertise. Comments on management of Italian companies include references to charisma and spontaneity and non-Italians claim that managers of Italian companies lack the necessary discipline in discharging their responsibilities.

For all of the national differences, and it is also impossible to make generalizations about a particular country given that social and economic conditions may vary from region-to-region within a specific national border, it appears to be true in general that European managerial styles are less formal than what is typically observed in the United States. Job

---

[13] Ronen, S., and O. Shenkar. 1985. "Clustering Countries on Attitudinal Dimensions: A Review and Synthesis." *Academy of Management Review* 10, no. 3, pp. 435–54.

descriptions and organizational charts in European companies are less detailed and specific than those used by US companies. European companies also tend to fall in the middle between the individualism prized by US companies and the strong group orientation found among Japanese companies. Similarly, business–government relations in Europe are less adversarial than in the United States yet one generally does not see government acting as a strong "guiding hand" along the lines of certain countries in Asian countries. Exceptions can be seen, however, in those countries such as France and Italy that have often given strong governmental support to certain domestic companies and industries. One interesting distinction in Europe is the degree of protection given to personal time and employment security, a value that is embedded in governmental regulation of vacation time and other personal leaves and lay-offs caused by mergers and internal corporate restructuring.

Asian Business Culture

Much of the earliest writing about Asian businesses emphasized and discussed management cultures within Japanese and Korean corporations, since these were the two countries that had the greatest initial success following World War II in entering global markets and challenging the previously assumed dominance of American and European management principles.[14] As is the case with companies around the world, the business culture preferred in Japan and Korea has often been indistinguishable from the dominant national cultural values and it is not surprising

---

[14] The discussion of Asian business culture in this section is adapted from Humes, S. 1993. *Managing the Multinational: Confronting the Global-Local Dilemma*, 116–18. Prentice Hall International (UK) Ltd. Hemel Hempstead, Hertfordshire UK. The existence of a recognizable Far Eastern business culture has been postulated for a cluster of Asian countries other than Japan (e.g., Hong Kong, Singapore, Taiwan, Thailand and Vietnam); however, the dynamic economic renaissance of Japan since the end of World War II has been such that most commentators treat Japanese management principals as an independent phenomenon separate from its geographic neighbors. See Ronen, S., and O. Shenkar. 1985. "Clustering Countries on Attitudinal Dimensions: A Review and Synthesis." *Academy of Management Review* 10, no. 3, pp. 435–54.

to see that multinational companies domiciled in these countries have emphasized consensus, seniority, and deference to authority. Executives and managers within Japanese and Korean corporations have typically been products of the broader class hierarchy within the national culture and drawn from a group of "elites" that have completed their education at leading universities at which they forged the social ties that follow them through the business careers. It is well known that, at least until quite recently, a bedrock principle within Japanese multinationals was lifetime employment that created unequivocal corporate loyalty among employees. Employees expected to spend their entire careers with one company and, as such, were willing to subordinate their personal ambitions and family lives to the needs of the company. In fact, the social status of managers and employees among their peers was strongly influenced by the company that they worked for and the position that they occupied within the company. Since Asian multinationals, particularly in Japan, generally did not welcome job candidates who had already spent part of their career at other companies, employees generally had no choice but to accept the decision made by their employers about their careers given that there was little or no chance they could move elsewhere in the event that they were not satisfied with their progress.

While the life of the typical Japanese employee often seemed to harken back to feudal times, Japanese companies did take some efforts to create a pleasant and fulfilling work environment. For example, Japanese employees have long been exposed to a constant stream of training and education to provide them with new skills and knowledge. A sense of belonging and connection is fostered through group exercises and company rituals as well as a focus on cooperation and harmony. While Japanese employees may not have had much real autonomy, they have nonetheless been included in the procedures used to discuss issues and problems and reach decisions that are agreeable to, and supported by, all persons directly involved in the matter. It should be noted, however, that while this time-consuming process, the so-called "ringi system," appeared to be more inclusive than the methods used in American and European companies, the fact is that the decisions were often made at the top and then politely but firmly explained and sold to those who are lower in the organizational hierarchy. One important byproduct of the internal socialization process in Japanese companies has been the development of shared cultural values that reduce the need for those companies to create detailed rules and procedures of the type relied on by US companies.

In contrast to the American preoccupation with specialization, management careers in Japanese companies have traditionally emphasized development of generalist skills. In fact, as a general matter all employees in Japanese companies are told that they are expected to work for the entire organization, as opposed to a particular functional or product division, and that they will be asked to perform a wide range of roles during their relationship with the company. Human resources policies and practices, and management development programs in particular, at Japanese companies reflect a commitment to long-term development and socialization of employees and this focus can be observed in the way that training programs are carried out and in the choices made with respect to ensuring that employees are rotated through a variety of assignments so that they can see how the business works from a number of perspectives. The willingness to make long-term investments in human resources is consistent with the way that Japanese companies and investors are willing to take a long-term view of financial performance as opposed to following the way of US companies in tracking on short-term results.

Cooperation and the desire to build and maintain a sense of community also has a powerful impact on business-government relations in many Asian economies. The important role of Japanese ministries and other governmental agencies in providing direction to domestic corporations and industry sectors is well documented. For example, governmental agencies in Japan have had broad authority and discretion with respect to granting licenses and other types of approvals that are necessary for the conduct of certain business activities and also have exerted substantial power to impact commercial activities by approving or denying subsidies, tax holidays and reductions, and/or loans on favorable terms. In addition, the Ministries of Finance and International Trade and Industry have both been known for their practices of issuing "administrative guidance" to domestic companies as a tool to ensure that Japanese firms were positioned to be competitive in international markets.

While much of the writing about Asian multinationals, and Japanese companies in particular, has created a perception that they are all quite similar, in fact one can observe striking differences in the way that major corporate groups are organized and in the cultural values that they choose to emphasize. For example, while the culture of the Mitsubishi group strongly emphasized the organization as a whole and the parent company exerted a strong role, the Mitsui group appeared to allow for a good deal of autonomy for its various divisions and affiliates. Also, not surprisingly, Japanese multinationals have adopted different strategies to achieve comparable objectives with respect to recruiting and developing competent international managers.

Interest in Asian business culture has obviously expanded beyond Japan and Korea and the existence of a recognizable Far Eastern business culture has been postulated for a cluster of Asian countries other than Japan (e.g., Hong Kong, Singapore, Taiwan, Thailand, and Vietnam); however, the dynamic economic renaissance of Japan after World War II has been such that most commentators have treated Japanese management principles as an independent phenomenon separate from its geographic neighbors.[15] A relatively recent phenomenon has been the emergence of Chinese companies as strong competitors in the global marketplace and the tighter engagement of American and European companies with China as a market for their products and services and a source of financial and human capital and technology. Certainly China and Japan share not only geographical proximity but also similar religions and value systems; however, their national business cultures have diverged significantly for various reasons including, perhaps most notably, differences in the path and content of their economic policies.[16]

---

[15] See Ronen, S., and O. Shenkar. 1985. "Clustering Countries on Attitudinal Dimensions: A Review and Synthesis." *Academy of Management Review* 10, no. 3, pp. 434–54.

[16] Padmalingam, S. April 2002. "Differences in Economic Policies of Japan and China and the Impact on their Respective Societies." http://econc10. bu.edu/economic_systems/Country_comparisons/japan_china3.htm (accessed December 31, 2018).

CHAPTER 4

Cross-Cultural Transfer of Management Theories

Introduction

Most of the research activities conducted in the field of comparative management studies have focused on identifying and explaining similarities and differences among various management systems. In addition, this field includes the pursuit of universally, or at least broadly, applicable management systems, philosophies, values, and practices that can be transferred effectively across cultures with predictable and desired results. The transfer is a complex process involving not only the technical aspects of a particular management system but also verification that the application of the principles associated with that system is having the desired behavioral impact in the specific cultural and environmental context in which the transfer is occurring. Given that much of the early research relating to issues addressed under the umbrella of management studies was carried out in the United States and/or abroad by US-oriented scholars, it is not surprising that a good deal of controversy has surrounded the cross-cultural transfer of US management theories. Recently, however, debate and research regarding cross-cultural transfer of management theories, styles, and practices perceived to be successful in one country has expanded to include transfers from countries other than the United States. For example, the economic prowess of Japanese multinationals during the 1970s and 1980s led to the proliferation of prescriptions for their challenged competitors in the United States and elsewhere to seriously consider importing and adapting Japanese management practices Another interesting development with respect to research regarding cross-cultural transfers of management styles and practice is that the United States is no longer always involved in the conversation, either as a transferor or a transferee. Kumar, for example, noted that India could expect a significant amount of investment from Japan, thus calling for an examination of how Japanese management practices would fare if they were applied in Indian subsidiaries.[1]

Hofstede on Cross-Cultural Transfer of US Management Theories

Hofstede was one of the first to argue that the leadership and management theories and practices used in a particular country, and the efficacy of those theories and practices, were significantly influenced by the attributes of the societal culture in that country.[2] Hofstede recognized that many of his colleagues had devoted their time and effort to uncovering and popularizing "universal" management principles that could be applied in every country regardless of the cultural dimensions that dominate in that country; however, his understanding of cultural dimensions led him to pursue the question of "[t]o what extent do theories developed in one country and reflecting the cultural boundaries of that country apply to other countries?"[3] Hofstede was quite clear about his belief that management theories reflect the cultural environmental in which they were written, whether the theories were developed in the United States or elsewhere, but given the dominance of US-oriented management theories at the time his model of cultural dimensions was first developed it was not surprising that Hofstede would turn his attention to whether certain well-known US theories of motivation, organizational structure,

---

[1] Kumar, R. n.d. "Comparative Research on Indian and Japanese Management Styles: Bridging Strategies to Bring them Closer." http://scribd.com/doc/29728070/Comparative-study-on-Indian-and-Japanese-management-style (accessed December 31, 2018) The paper also includes a review of the literature relating to both Japanese and Indian management styles and a comparison between them based on Hofstede's cultural dimensions.

[2] Hofstede, G. 1980. "Motivation, Leadership and Organization: Do American Theories Apply Abroad." *Organization Dynamics* 9, no. 1, pp. 42–63, 49 and 50.

[3] Id. at 50.

and managerial style (i.e., "management by objectives") could be readily applied in other countries with different societal culture characteristics.[4]

Theories of motivation

For Hofstede, the key question with respect to motivation was: "Why do people behave as they do?" He took note of a number of theories of human motivation including the work of psychologists such as Sigmund Freud and US management theorists such as David McClelland, Abraham Maslow, Frederick Herzberg, and Victor Vroom.[5] Each of those theories provide interesting, if not simplistic and vague, insights into what factors motivate people in the workplace and valuable information on what managers might focus upon in their efforts to control the activities of their subordinates in a way that is calculated to obtain the results thought to be necessary for the firm to be successful. Hofstede noted that acceptance of particular theories leads to specific assumptions about the role of managers. For example, Vroom's expectancy theory implies, at least in part, that employees can be pulled to take certain actions by creating a reasonable expectancy of desired rewards from those actions and the job for managers therefore is to device systems that align performance with outcomes ("rewards") that are valued by employees; however, Freud's theories assumed that employees were being pushed by internal forces, often unconsciously, which were extremely difficult for managers to identify, understand, and overcome.[6]

---

[4] Hofstede also discussed and critiqued the applicability of several of the most well-known US-originated "participative leadership" theories such as McGregor's Theory X and Theory Y, Likert's System Four management model and Blake and Mouton's Managerial Grid.

[5] Hofstede, G. 1980. "Motivation, Leadership and Organization: Do American Theories Apply Abroad." *Organization Dynamics* 9, no. 1, pp. 42–53. Adler also examined the same US-based motivation theories in her research regarding cross-cultural differences in managerial practices with respect to motivation. See Adler, N. 1991. *International Dimensions of Organizational Behavior*, 14–178, 2nd ed. Boston: PWS-Kent Publishing Co.

[6] Hofstede, G. 1980. "Motivation, Leadership and Organization: Do American Theories Apply Abroad." *Organization Dynamics* 9, no. 1, pp. 42–63, 53.

Hofstede argued that the popularity and efficacy of theories of motivation in a particular country depends not only upon the cultural dimensions in that country but also the cultural dimensions in the country where the particular theory was first developed. He considered the question of why Freud's theories have never been accepted as an integral part of US-developed management theories by analyzing the cultural profile of Austria, where Freud lived and worked as part of the middle class as his ideas about human motivation emerged, to demonstrate both why Freudian thinking was popular in Austria and out of step with the dominant cultural dimensions in the United States.[7] Hofstede noted that Freud was a product of the late 19th and early 20th centuries, during which time he developed and refined most of his theories; however, Hofstede suggested that cultural patterns change relatively slowly and that it was likely that the fundamental aspects of the cultural dimensions of Austria at the time of the Hofstede survey were much the same as they had been 70 or 80 years before.[8] He then compared and contrasted the United States and Austria on each of four cultural dimensions and found that power distance and individualism were both much lower in Austria while uncertainty avoidance and masculinity were both much higher in Austria. For Hofstede, one of the most compelling findings from his survey regarding Austria was the combination of high uncertainty avoidance with low power distance since, in general, countries with a strong aversion to risk tended to gravitate toward a high power distance and place their trust in strong superiors to take control and manage uncertainties for everyone by establishing formal rules and espousing absolute truths that were to be

---

[7] Id.

[8] Hofstede's view is that cultural change that is significant enough to invalidate his country dimension index rankings will take a significant period of time, such as 50 to 100 years, or the occurrence of a dramatic outside event of epic proportions and he believes that cultural differences between countries identified in the IBM studies could already be observed from information about conditions and values in those countries hundreds of years before. See Hofstede, G. 2006. "Dimensionalizing Cultures: The Hofstede Model in Context." In *Online Readings in Psychology and Culture, Unit 2: Conceptual, Methodological and Ethical Issues in Psychology and Culture*, eds. W.J. Lonner, D.L. Dinnel, S.A. Hayes, and D.N. Sattler. Bellingham, WA: Center for Cross Cultural Research.

blindly followed.[9] Hofstede argued that reference could be made to Freudian theories to explain how Austrians, as well people in other countries with the same combination of scores on these two cultural dimensions (e.g., Finland, Germany, Israel, and Switzerland), coped with their aversion to risk without a strong "external boss." His view was that Austrians relied on what Freud referred to as the Superego to continuously monitor and evaluate the behavior of their Ego against an ideal standard thus, in effect, acting as their own superior.[10] Hofstede also noted that Austrians, who scored low on individualism, had a strong sense of national identity, which drove them to work hard out of a strong feeling of obligation to their country and fellow citizens.[11]

Hofstede also argued that his survey results with respect to the United States could explain why the other non-Freudian theories relating to motivation, which he referred to generally as "expectancy" theories, achieved a high level of recognition and acceptance in that country. The combination of weak uncertainty avoidance and strong masculinity was found exclusively in the United States, in other countries in the Anglo-American group and in some of their former colonies. Hofstede cited a strong relationship between the grouping of countries in this quadrant and countries found to evidence a high need for achievement by other researchers

---

[9] Japan as well as all of the Latin and Mediterranean countries in the Hofstede survey fell into the large power distance/strong uncertainty avoidance quadrant. Hofstede, G. 1980. "Motivation, Leadership and Organization: Do American Theories Apply Abroad." *Organization Dynamics* 9, no. 1, pp. 42–63, 51 and 53.

[10] According to Freud, human behavior is influenced by the "Id," "Ego," and "Superego": the Id includes unconscious forces within each person that drive them to act in a certain way; the Ego is a person's conscious conception of himself or herself that is constantly struggling to control the Id; and the Superego is an unconscious "internal pilot" developed through early socialization mainly through one's parents that criticizes the thoughts and actions of the Ego and produces guilt and anxiety whenever the Ego appears to be giving in to the Id. Freud's theory is quite complex and this description is necessarily simplistic. For an introduction to the details, see Freud, S. 1990. *The Ego and the Id (The Standard Edition of the Complete Psychological Works of Sigmund Freud)*. New York, NY: W.W. Norton & Company.

[11] Hofstede, G. 1980. "Motivation, Leadership and Organization: Do American Theories Apply Abroad." *Organization Dynamics* 9, no. 1, pp. 42–63, 51 and 53.

such as McClelland, who is one of the noted US management theorists in area of motivation.[12] Hofstede observed correlations between the beliefs that are most likely to be seen in weak uncertainty avoidance and strongly masculine societies and the writings of McClelland and US theorists on the motives behind the actions taken by persons in those societies. For example, Hofstede argued that McClelland's "achievement motive"[13] was only viable in a cultural context where persons were willing to accept at least a moderate level of risk and were also concerned about performance (i.e., weak uncertainty avoidance/masculine societies).[14] The logical corollary to this argument is that management practices based on the assumption that people behave in accordance with the "achievement motive" would not be successful in countries where there is a great concern with

---

[12] Id. at 55. McClelland identified "need for achievement scores" in a number of countries based on survey data collected for both 1925 and 1950. McClelland, D.C. 1961. *The Achieving Society*. Princeton, NJ: D. Van Nostrand. Hofstede noted that the countries in the weak uncertainty avoidance/masculine quadrant received mostly high achievement need scores while countries in the strong uncertainty avoidance/feminine quadrant scored on at the lower end of the range in the McClelland survey. Hofstede also observed that the very word "achievement" is difficult to translate into any language other than English and that he could not use the word in the questionnaire relied upon in his own research because it could not be readily understood in many of the countries in his survey group. The English-speaking countries in the Hofstede survey all appeared in the weak uncertainty avoidance/masculine quadrant. Hofstede, G. 1980. "Motivation, Leadership and Organization: Do American Theories Apply Abroad." *Organization Dynamics* 9, no. 1, pp. 42–63, 55.

[13] McClelland claimed that humans act out of a need to achieve, which he referred to as the "achievement motive." See McClelland, D.C. 1953. *The Achievement Motive*. New York, NY: Appleton-Century. Crofts, and Power. 1975. *The Inner Experience*, New York, NY: Irvington, and 1987. *Human Motivation*. Cambridge, UK: Cambridge University Press.

[14] Hofstede, G. 1980. "Motivation, Leadership and Organization: Do American Theories Apply Abroad." *Organization Dynamics* 9, no. 1, pp. 42–63, 55. In countries where uncertainty avoidance is weak, there is more willingness within society to take risks in life. In strongly masculine societies, performance is what counts, money and things are important and are to be pursued, the drive for work and success is fueled by ambition, and those who achieve success are admired and praised.

security in life, competition is looked upon with disapproval, and motivation is provided by the desire to be of service rather by a need to attain greater levels of wealth and fame (i.e., countries appearing in the strong uncertainty avoidance/feminine quadrant). Care should be taken not to make assumptions based on observation of a single cultural element since a strong urge to work hard can be a sign of both a strong drive for achievement and an attempt to somehow manage and reduce risk and insecurity.

Hofstede also discussed how the information from his study might call into question the universality of the hierarchy of human needs proposed by Maslow.[15] Hofstede focused on the four quadrants of the cultural map that had masculinity and uncertainty avoidance as its two dimensional axis and described what he believed was the correlation between each quadrant and the hierarchical levels of the Maslow model:

- The weak uncertainty avoidance/masculine quadrant, which was exclusively populated by the United States, other countries in the Anglo-American group and some of their former colonies, was consistent with Maslow's fourth hierarchical level: esteem needs (i.e., self-esteem, confidence, performance, achievement and respect from others).
- The strong uncertainty avoidance/masculine quadrant includes countries that also value performance and hard work, as do those countries in the weak uncertainty avoidance/masculine quadrant; however, the primary objective of these behaviors in these countries is security (i.e., the management and reduction of risk), which is Maslow's second hierarchical level.

---

[15] Id. at 55–56. Under Maslow's famous hierarchy of human needs persons behave in a rational fashion to satisfy five levels of needs running from "basic" to "higher" in the following successive fashion—psychological needs; safety or security needs; social needs; esteem needs; and self-actualization needs. A higher need will not be an active concern for a person until he or she has sufficiently satisfied each of the lower needs. See Maslow, A.H. 1943. "A Theory of Human Motivation." *Psychological Review* 50, no. 4, 370–96. See also Maslow, A.H. 1943. *Motivation and Personality*. New York, NY: Harper, and Maslow, A.H. 1998. *Maslow on Management*. New York, NY Wiley.

- The two quadrants for which feminine values were higher each include countries in which quality of life and interpersonal relationships are more important than performance, money and collecting symbols of wealth and achievement. Although risk tolerance, measured by uncertainty avoidance, varied between these two quadrants, Hofstede argued that Maslow's third hierarchical level, social needs (i.e., friendship, family, sexual intimacy, quality of life), were most important to all of these more feminine countries.

Hofstede, noting that Maslow placed esteem/achievement needs above social and security needs in his ideal hierarchical structure, argued that the Maslow model could not be a universally true description of the human motivation process in light of the information regarding cultural values previously outlined and was instead a description of the prevailing value system in Maslow's home country (United States). Hofstede explained that continued reference to some of sort of hierarchy of human needs would only be meaningful if the levels were rearranged for countries in each of the quadrants to recognize their specific needs and cultural values. Therefore, for those countries in the strong uncertainty avoidance/masculine quadrant, such as Japan and Latin and Mediterranean countries such as Argentina, Columbia, Italy, Mexico, and Venezuela, security needs would be a higher priority; for those countries in the weak uncertainty/feminine quadrant, such as the Scandinavian countries and the Netherlands, social needs would rank at the top of the hierarchy; and for those countries in the strong uncertainty avoidance/feminine quadrant, a diverse geographically dispersed group including Brazil, France, Israel, Portugal, and Taiwan among others, both social and security (due to the high level of risk intolerance) needs would be the most important.[16]

Motivation in the workplace is obviously a complex topic and there have been a number of ideas about how firms can improve attitudes of workers and thus motivate to engage in the behaviors desired by the management. Hofstede referred to two proposals, which he placed under the

---

[16] Hofstede, G. 1980. "Motivation, Leadership and Organization: Do American Theories Apply Abroad." *Organization Dynamics* 9, no. 1, pp. 42–63, 55–56.

general umbrella of "humanization of work" that were becoming quite popular at the time that Hofstede began publishing on the results of his initial survey: job enrichment, which has been credited to Herzberg and seeks to motivate employees by allowing them to have more responsibility and variety in their jobs[17] and the formation of autonomous work groups ("teams") with almost complete autonomy to decide upon the best way to achieve specific goals assigned to the team by senior management. Hofstede speculated that the origin of these proposals reflected the cultural values of their chief proponents and that the efficacy of the proposals would be determined by how well they fit with societal beliefs about just what made a particular job "human." As for job enrichment, Hofstede felt that it would take flight more easily in more masculine countries such as the United States since individual performance was more important in those societies.[18] In contrast, teams seemed to be a better fit for feminine

---

[17] Herzberg distinguished between motivator and hygienic factors. His motivator factors are similar to Maslow's "higher" esteem and self-actualization needs and include achievement. recognition, responsibility, promotion, growth, and fulfilling work activities. His hygienic factors are similar to Maslow's three lowest/most basic levels—psychological, safety, and social—and include pay and benefits, personal life, work conditions, job security, status, relations with coworkers, and supervisors and company policies and administrative procedures. See Herzberg, F. 1959. *The Motivation to Work*. New York, NY: John Wiley & Sons. Job enrichment was one of the strategies that hopefully would serve as a motivator by allowing workers to find more satisfaction, and increase their motivation to perform, by introducing skill variety, task identity, task significance, autonomy, and feedback.

[18] While job enrichment would appear, on the face of it, to be a positive initiative in a cultural environment such as the United States it is not necessarily the best approach in all instances. As one commentator noted: "... [j]ob enrichment doesn't work for everyone. Some people are very resistant to more responsibility or to opportunities for personal growth, but…researchers report that some people they expected to resist, seized the opportunity. Enriching jobs is a particularly effective way to develop employees provided the jobs are truly enriched, not just more work for them to do." See Brown, R. April 22, 2010. "Design Jobs that Motivate and Develop People." http://media-associates.co.nz/index.php?option=com_content&view=article&id=26:design-jobs-that-motivate-and-develop-people&catid=4:free&Itemid=21

societies where humanization was realized through creating more opportunities for wholesome interpersonal relationships while downplaying
competition among individuals in the workplace.[19] In fact, one of the first
companies to experiment with the use of autonomous work teams was
Volvo in Sweden, which had the highest femininity score in the survey
group, where teams had the right to determine all of the key aspects associated with the activities of the team and particular job responsibilities
including work assignments, schedules, and quality control procedures.
Many teams functioned without formal supervisors and decision were to
be made democratically with each team member shouldering leadership
of the group and providing input on decisions about strategies and allo-
cations of resources.[20]

Theories of Organization

Two of the fundamental issues relating to organizational structure are
the degree to which authority for decisions can be comfortably delegated to lower levels within the hierarchy—centralization versus decentralization—and the level of reliance on formal rules and specialization.
Hofstede argued that the position of a country on his power distance/
uncertainty avoidance cultural map could provide important clues as
to what type of organizational structure would be most effective in that
country. He asserted that, in general, managers and subordinates in larger
power distance countries preferred and expected that responsibility for
launching new initiatives and making decisions would be centralized and
placed near the top of the organizational hierarchy[21] while persons in

---

[19] Hofstede, G. 1980. "Motivation, Leadership and Organization: Do American
Theories Apply Abroad." *Organization Dynamics* 9, no. 1, pp. 42–63, 56.
[20] *Encyclopedia of Business*, 2d—Teams. April 22, 2010. http://referenceforbusi-
ness.com/encyclopedia/Str-The/Teams.html
[21] Hofstede provided an example of country differences based on power distance by contrasting what he referred to as the standard practice among medium
power distance US multinationals of having salary increase proposals initiated by
the direct superior of the impacted employee to the process followed in French
firms of requiring that such proposals must be initiated by superiors several levels
removed and above the impacted employee after information is delivered upward

small power distance countries, both managers and subordinates, would be more comfortable with decentralization.[22] With regard to formalities and rulemaking, Hofstede believed that the stronger the level of uncertainty avoidance the more likely it would be that one would find highly formalized systems since rules and procedures are seen as appropriate tools to manage uncertainty and alleviate stress and anxiety.[23]

Hofstede cited a then unpublished work of one of his colleagues as a source of interesting insight on how a country's placement along the dimensions of power distance and uncertainty avoidance might predict the preferences of firms from those countries with respect to the centralization and formality in their organizational structures and, in turn, the processes used by those firms to identify and resolve problems that might arise during day-to-day operations. His colleague surveyed graduate business students from three different European countries—France, Germany, and Great Britain—and asked them for ideas about how to deal

---

through the appropriate channels. Hofstede explained that in large power distance countries such as France, even superiors are strongly dependent on their own superiors and thus middle managers are more comfortable referring decisions upward and, in fact, employees in those countries expect that this will be the process that is followed and generally do not object. See Hofstede, G. 1980. "Motivation, Leadership and Organization: Do American Theories Apply Abroad?" *Organization Dynamics* 9, no. 1, p. 42–63, 59–60.

[22] Id. at 59. Related to the decision regarding the appropriate degree of decentralization is the number of hierarchical levels in the organizational structure—organizations with more levels are referred to as "tall" while organizations with fewer levels are referred to as "flat" and are inclined to accept and embrace decentralization since power distances are, by definition, smaller. It would be expected that organizations in large power distance cultures would be taller with more layers (i.e., more hierarchical) and that the chain of command would be a more important element of the decision-making processes in those organizations. See also Schwartz, S.H. 1999. "A Theory of Cultural Values and Some Implications for Work." *Applied Psychology: An International Review* 48, no. 1, pp. 23–47 (distinguishing cultures on a continuum between hierarchical and egalitarian and noting importance of hierarchical organizational structures and chain of authority in hierarchical cultures).

[23] Hofstede, G. 1980. "Motivation, Leadership and Organization: Do American Theories Apply Abroad?" *Organization Dynamics* 9, no. 1, pp. 42–63, 60.

with issues in a case study that involved a conflict between the product development and sales departments at a hypothetical firm. Interestingly, most of the students from France advised that resolution of the conflict required attention and intervention from the highest level of the organizational hierarchy (i.e., the president); however, the Germans and British had other ideas about the reasons for the problem and the suggested solution—the Germans pointed to a lack of written policies to guide each of the departments and recommended that such policies be drafted while the British felt that the conflict was a product of poor interpersonal communication that required more training for the parties involved.[24]

Based on these results, Hofstede's colleague proposed "implicit models" of organization for the three countries and other countries that occupied the same quadrant with them on the cultural map that had uncertainty avoidance and power distance as its two-dimensional axis. For French firms (large power distance/strong uncertainty avoidance), the preferred organizational structure resembled a pyramid and responsibility and authority for making decisions was centralized, and the rules of operation were formalized. German firms (small power distance/strong uncertainty avoidance) strived for a "well-oiled machine" efficiently directed by formal procedures although not necessarily centralized. Hofstede noted that this was consistent with the views of the well-known German management theorist Max Weber, whose theory of bureaucracy included a high level of formalization in management systems but with rules that were intended to protect persons at lower levels in the hierarchical structure from attempts by their superior to abuse their power.[25] British firms (small power distance/weak uncertainty avoidance) tended to opt for what was referred to as a "village market" that was neither formalized nor centralized. As for the four Asian countries—Hong Kong, India, the

---

[24] Hofstede was referring to the work of O.J. Stevens at INSTEAD. Id. at 60.

[25] According to Weber's theory of bureaucracy, persons in a position of authority within the organizational structure did not have power in their own right but could give directions that were consistent with the authority vested in their position in the formal written rules and procedures that described the approved management systems for the firm. In short, as Hofstede said, "the power is in the role, not in the person (small Power Distance)". Id.

Philippines, and Singapore—in the remaining quadrant of the cultural map (large power distance/weak uncertainty avoidance). Hofstede suggested that the appropriate implicit model of organization should be the "family," which he described as centralized with respect to how and by whom decisions are made and formalized with respect to relationships among persons within the hierarchy (large power distance) but not overly formalized as to the rulemaking on how the day-to-day workflow is conducted (weak uncertainty avoidance).[26]

Hofstede noted that the United States could be found in the middle of the uncertainty avoidance/power distance cultural map and suggested that this provided an explanation as to why US firms doing business outside their domestic borders could readily adapt to each of the "implicit models" described earlier. For example, when operating in France a local subsidiary of a US company operating with local manages and personnel might use the pyramid model and formulate more formal rules and procedures than would be the case in the United States. This approach would be followed not because hierarchies and rules are goals in and of themselves, as might be the case with a truly French firm, but as a means for accomplishing the business and strategic objective of establishing an efficient and productive subsidiary in France using local human resources.[27] Hofstede also suggested that the preferred implicit model for a particular country could predict the likelihood that firms and managers from those countries would experiment with various temporary and flexible organizational structures such as the "matrix." For example, the relatively pragmatic attitudes of US firms toward the value and use of hierarchical structures and bureaucratic processes could explain why they were more likely to implement matrix organizational structures while French and German managers could be expected to be uncomfortable with the matrix based on what they perceive to be a lack of a clear chain of command and organizational clarity.[28]

---

[26] Id.

[27] Id.

[28] Id. at 60–61. Hofstede noted, however, that there were instances of French and German firms where the matrix structure had been used successfully and argued that cultural barriers and skepticism could be overcome by careful planning and

At least two studies appear to confirm the assumptions made by Hofstede with respect to the relationship between power distance and reliance upon formal rules and procedures to provide guidance on carrying out day-to-day activities.[29] In both cases, the researchers found that managers in large power distance countries were more likely than their colleagues in small power distance countries to use formal rules and procedures that were established at the top of the organizational hierarchy to direct subordinates and that those managers were also more likely to rely on their own experiences when making decisions about everyday activities and issues without seeking and considering the views and opinions of their subordinates.

Another interesting finding with regard to power distance is the impact that it appears to have on how organizational support for innovation is pursued. One group of researchers has found evidence that people working within organizations in large power distance countries prefer that persons looking to gain support for a new product or idea, the so-called innovation champions, go first to those in authority for review and approval as opposed to trying to build a groundswell of support from the "bottom-up" by eliciting interest and excitement from members working at lower levels in the hierarchical structure of the organization. As power distance gets smaller, however, there is greater acceptance and tolerance of proactive innovation efforts by persons at any level in the hierarchy.[30]

---

implementation such as working to ensure that the organizational role of each person is unambiguously defined and formal procedures are put in place at the beginning to resolve conflicts that may arise in the matrix structure due to the dual reporting relationships that will exist.

[29] Smith, P.B., M.F. Peterson, and S.H. Schwarz. 2002. "Cultural Values, Sources of Guidance, and their Relevance to Managerial Behavior—A 47-Nation Study." *Journal of Cross-Cultural Psychology* 33, no. 2, pp. 188–208; Smith, P., M. Peterson, and J. Misumi. 1994. "Event Management and Work Team Effectiveness in Japan, Britain and the USA." *Journal of Occupational and Organizational Psychology* 67, no. 1, pp. 33–43.

[30] Shane, S., S. Venkataraman and I. MacMillan. 1995. "Cultural Differences in Innovation Championing Roles." *Journal of Management* 21, no. 5, pp. 931–52.

Management by Objectives

Hofstede also commented on how well one might expect Drucker's well-known management by objectives (MBO) to be accepted in cultural environments other than the United States.[31] In brief, MBO, which was first introduced by Drucker in the 1950s and was much discussed during the time that Hofstede first released his survey results, is based on the principle that individual efforts must be put together to achieve a common goal known to, and accepted by, everyone in the organization and required the completion of the following steps: organizational objectives must be defined at the very top of the hierarchy, such as the board level; management roles and activities should be analyzed to that duties and responsibilities relating to achievement of the objectives can be properly allocated among the individual managers; performance standards should be established; managers and subordinates should agree upon and define specific objectives for the activities of the subordinates; the targets set for each subordinate should be aligned with the larger objectives of the organization; and management information systems should be created to monitor performance and the actual relationship of individual achievement to organizational objectives.

Hofstede argued that, not surprisingly, several of the assumptions underlying MBO could be traced to cultural dimensions that were comfortable for the United States. First of all, MBO, which contemplates a good deal of dialogue between organizational units, and managers and subordinates, regarding objectives, targets, and standards assumes that subordinates have sufficient independence and confidence to engage in meaningful negotiations with persons higher in the organizational hierarchy (i.e., small or medium power distance). Second, MBO assumes that everyone in the organization, subordinates and their managers, is willing to take risks (i.e., weak uncertainty avoidance). Finally, MBO assumes that subordinates and managers all believe that performance, as measured by achievement of organizational goals and related individual targets, is important (i.e., high masculinity). He then discussed how well MBO might be received in countries with a different cultural profile.

---

[31] Drucker, P. 1954. *The Practice of Management*. New York, NY Harper & Row.

In Germany, for example, Hofstede noted that its small power distance should support and welcome dialogue within the organization regarding goals and objectives, but that problems might arise with respect to acceptance of risk given that Germany is a much stronger uncertainty avoidance society.[32] Attempts to implement MBO in France were a failure in Hofstede's view because France is a large power distance society in which managers are uncomfortable with decentralizing authority and subordinates do not expect managers to delegate authority and, in fact, prefer that managers provide direction through a hierarchical structure that reduces stress and anxiety by its very predictability.[33]

Harris and Moran

The ability of a manager to communicate and direct effectively in another country depends in large part on the manager's understanding of the local societal culture and the way that it influences expectations regarding the relationship between managers and subordinates in the workplace. It is generally understood and explained that societal culture depends on economic, legal, and political factors as well as sociocultural factors

---

[32] Hofstede, G. 1980. "Motivation, Leadership and Organization: Do American Theories Apply Abroad." *Organization Dynamics* 9, no. 1, pp. 42–63, 58. Hofstede does point out that MBO can fit well with German small power distance/strong uncertainty avoidance to the extent that mutually agreed upon objectives provide subordinates with direction that alleviates stress while also removing the threat of arbitrary authority exercised by superiors. Hofstede cites studies of the use of MBO in German-speaking countries that illustrate a preference for the elaborate formal information systems suggested by Drucker and an emphasis on group objectives that is consistent with the low individualism values in these countries. Id.

[33] Id. at 58–59. Initially it was thought that MBO might be a means for implementing what some believed was a long overdue democratization of management processes within French organizations; however, the cultural aversion to participatory management practices, shared by persons at all levels of the organizational hierarchy, proved too difficult to overcome in most instances and Hofstede reported that the French version of MBO—referred to as DPPO (Direction Participative par Objectifs)—had largely been discredited by the time that he first published his survey results at the end of the 1970s. Id.

including religion and language. Harris and Moran were more specific when they identified eight categories or subsystems of variables that they argued should be analyzed in order to develop a comprehensive profile of a particular societal culture[34]:

- Kinship—guides family relationships
- Education—formal or informal education of workers affects workplace expectations
- Economy—means of production and distribution in a society influences all aspects of the resource allocation
- Politics—system of government imposes varying constraints on an organization
- Religion—spiritual beliefs of a society are so powerful that they overpower all other cultural aspects
- Associations—the formal and informal groups that make up a society
- Health—system of health care affects employee productivity
- Recreation—the use, attitude, and choice of how to use leisure time

All these factors and variables combine and work together to provide the context for the emergence of a societal culture that consists of a set of beliefs, values, attitudes, and assumptions that are shared by a significant number of people. These elements of societal culture are important determinants of the basic attitudes and orientations of people in the society, including managers and employees, toward work, time, materialism, individualism, and change and these attitudes must be understood by managers so they can take into account the expectations of employees and develop managerial styles and practices that will motivate employees

---

[34] The list and description of Harris and Moran's eight categories or subsystems of variables is adapted from Blanchard, K., and A. Abdullah. 2006. "Chapter 3: Understanding the Role of Culture, Power Point Presentation, Prentice Hall, Classes." uleth.ca/200802/mgt3650n/CHAP03PP.PPT

to perform their jobs in ways that achieve the outcomes desired by the managers and the entire organization.[35]

Harris and Moran set out to illustrate some of the potential difficulties that US-centric managers might have when attempting to perform various managerial functions and roles in a different cultural environment and/or simply engaging in "arms-length" business relationships with their counterparts from other countries.[36] They began by providing the following list of various aspects of US culture (i.e., beliefs, values, attitudes, and assumptions that were shared by a significant number of people):

- The individual can influence the future ("where there is a will there is a way").
- The individual can change and improve the environment; an individual should be realistic in his or her aspirations.
- We must work hard to accomplish our objectives (the "Puritan work ethic").
- Commitments should be honored and people should/will do what they say they will do.
- One should effectively use one's time ("time is money" and thus can be saved or wasted).
- A primary obligation of an employee is to his or her organization.
- The employer or the employee can terminate the employment relationship.
- The best-qualified people should be given the available positions.

Harris and Moran also summarized key elements or characteristics of US culture that profiled Americans as goal and achievement oriented, highly organized and institutionally minded, freedom-loving and

---

[35] Id.

[36] The following discussion of the ideas of Harris and Moran is adapted from Harris, P., and R. Moran. 2000. *Managing Cultural Differences*, 5th ed. Houston TX: Gulf Publishing Company.

self-reliant, work oriented and efficient, friendly and informal, competitive and aggressive, and generous.

Harris and Moran then suggested the following list of alternative views to certain aspects of traditional US cultural beliefs, values, attitudes, and assumptions:

- Life follows a preordained course and human action is determined by the will of God.
- People are intended to adjust to the physical environment rather than alter it.
- Ideals are to be pursued regardless of what is "reasonable."
- Hard work is not the only prerequisite for success; wisdom, luck and time are also required.
- A commitment can be superseded by a conflict request, or an agreement may only signify intention and have little or no relationship to the capacity for performance.
- Schedules are important but only in relation to other priorities.
- The individual employee has a primary obligation to his or her family and friends.
- Employment is for a lifetime.
- Family, friendship, and other considerations should determine employment practices.

Having laid out two contrasting cultural visions of the world, Harris and Moran provided a few illustrations of potential problems for US managers operating abroad:

Planning: US managers are likely to rely heavily on scheduling and developing and implementing short- and long-term plans due to their belief that individuals can influence the future and that time is a scarce resource that is valued and thus needs to be carefully managed to avoid waste. In contrast, however, people from other cultures may avoid planning and/ or routinely ignore schedules because the fundamentally believe that the future is out of their hands, thus making planning a meaningless exercise, and that schedules are always subject to change if other priorities demand.

Motivation and Reward Systems: US managers are likely to bring an egalitarian perspective to motivational strategies and decisions regarding rewards in the relationship due to the influence of the Puritan work ethic, the belief that rewards should be given to the employees with the best qualifications and performance record, and the understanding that disenchanted employees are free to terminate the relationship at any time. People in other cultures, however, may have very different ideas about reward systems in the workplace and may place greater value on things other than hard work and productivity including wisdom, longevity, and familial/friendship relations.

Control: US managers are used to working in situations where their ability to control activities within their department or larger business unit is grounded in the fundamental expectation that employees will be honest and realistic in making their commitments to the organization; commitments, once made, will be honored; and employees will make their commitments to the organization a priority in their lives since a primary obligation of an employee is to his or her organization. However, people operating under alternative cultural values may cause frustrations to US managers because they tend to be more idealistic than realistic in making their commitments, thus setting the stage for failure, and are more prone than US persons to allowing commitments to be superseded by conflicting requests and to allowing obligations to family and friends to get in the way of their duties to their organization.

Transfer of Japanese Management Theories to the United States

While much of the debate among scholars of management studies has focused on the transferability of US management theories to other countries with different societal cultures, it has become clear that the United States does not have a monopoly on management ideas. It is well known that the success of Japanese firms in the United States and other Western markets during the 1980s and early 1990s led to a great deal of interest in examining whether Western companies could and should adopt certain managerial practices that appeared to be responsible for the growth and profitability of their Japanese competitors.[37] Conclusions among the experts have been mixed: some argue that Japanese managerial techniques are not transferable because they are based on unique cultural elements found only in Japan while others have claimed that these techniques can indeed be transferred and provided illustrations of how companies in the United States and Europe have successfully integrated strategies borrowed from Japan such as "quality circles" and "just-in-time" management.[38]

Linowes identified and described a "cultural divide" between the United States and Japan that would likely cause difficulties for Japanese managers attempting to operate and oversee subordinates in the United States.[39] Linowes suggested three points of differentiation. First, the Japanese managers tended toward patience and caution while action, risk-taking and bold initiatives were expected in the United States. Second, harmony, consensus building, conformity, and group convention were fundamental principles for the Japanese while those in the United States valued freedom, individuality, "being heard," and operating within a sort of "chaotic anarchy." Finally, while hierarchy based on loyalty and rewarding seniority was a long-standing tenant of Japanese organizational design and culture, persons in the United States had grown to expect equality in the workplace, which included broad opportunities for training and advancement, a "level-playing field" and reward systems based on performance.

The real answer regarding transferability of Japanese management techniques to the United States probably lies somewhere in the middle and recognizes that the content and utility of management techniques are always bound by cultural conditions to some extent and that some techniques simply cannot be transferred from culture to culture unless there is a conductive cultural environment in the society where the techniques

---

[37] See, e.g., Schein, E. 1981. "Does Japanese Management Style Have a Message for American Managers?" *Sloan Management Review* 23, no. 1, pp. 55–67.

[38] C. Johnson, "Japanese-Style Management in America." *California Management Review* 30, no. 4, pp. 34–45.

[39] Linowes, R.G. "The Japanese Manager's Traumatic Entry into the United States: Understanding the American–Japanese Cultural Divide." *The Academy of Management Executive* 7, no. 4, p. 24.

are being introduced. For example, Culpan and Kucukemiroglu predicted that the Japanese *ringi* system and the paternalistic orientation found in Japanese companies would not transfer well to a country such as the United States where individualism and privacy are highly valued.[40] However, they speculated that "a paternalistic approach, if modified to accommodate American cultural values, can be used by American managers to enhance employee commitment and involvement" and noted that the "open communication" techniques used in Japanese companies would be welcomed in the United States as a means of encouraged the increased sense of involvement craved by most US employees.[41]

---

[40] Culpan, R., and O. Kucukemiroglu. 1993. "A Comparison of US and Japanese Management Styles and Unit Effectiveness." *Management International Review* 33, 27–42.

[41] Id. See also Cool, K., and C. Lengnick-Hall. January 1985. "Second Thoughts on the Transferability of the Japanese Management Style." *Organization Studies* 6, pp. 1–22.

CHAPTER 5

Research on Management in Developing Countries

Introduction

For decades the general consensus among Western policy makers involved with international economic development was that real progress was dependent on making sure that poorer countries implemented and followed "appropriate" fiscal, monetary, trade, and legal practices. While there is little dispute that national economic policies and rules are important for economic development, it has also been recognized that the managers in developing countries that have a hand in producing goods and services can have just as much impact on the pace of development.[1] It is, therefore, essential to study and understand management practices and styles in developing countries; however, while developing countries represent an overwhelmingly large percentage of the world's population, the relatively small portion of global business activities in those countries, as well as other factors, has led to a small and spotty body of research on management practices and styles in those countries. One researcher lamented that while "[d]eveloping countries offer potentially some of the most important growth opportunities for companies both from the developing as the developing world Î [reviews] Î of empirical research grounded in institutional theory [have] found that most studies focused

---

[1] For an early discussion of the debate regarding the importance of "economists" versus "businesspeople" in fostering economic development, see Heller, F. 1968. "The Role of Management in Economic Development." *Management International Review* 8, no. 6, pp. 63–70.

on developed countries and that only a small portion of the studies tried to test institutional theory in developed countries."[2]

The field of management studies was conceived and developed predominantly in the United States, with some recent inputs coming from other industrialized countries in Europe and Asia (e.g., the tremendous interest in researching Japanese management practices in the 1980s and early 1990s). As such, most of management-related theories that have been produced and researched are based on circumstances in developed countries and thus include biases and assumptions that will likely make them inapplicable in developing countries. One of the problems with studying management in developing countries is that the landscape is tremendously diverse and includes countries of all sizes and from all continents and peoples who with unique histories that practice numerous religions, speak hundreds of different languages, and live in a breathtaking sweep of geographic conditions. All of this makes it difficult to formulate accurate and useful generalizations about "developing country management practices" and/or the attitudes and preferences of employees in all of those countries as to how they would like to be managed.

Applicability of Western Management Theories to Developing Countries

One of the long-running issues within the research community focusing on developing countries has been the extent to which management theories and practices with roots in the industrialized world could be understood and effectively applied by organizational managers in

---

[2] de Waal, A. 2007. "Is Performance Management Applicable in Developing Countries?: The case of a Tanzanian College." *International Journal of Emerging Markets* 2, no. 1, pp. 68–83, 68 (citing Farashahi, M., T. Hafso, and R. Molz. 2005. "Institutionalized Norms of Conducting Research and Social Realities: A Research Synthesis of Empirical Works from 1983 to 2002." *International Journal of Management Review* 7, no. 1, pp. 1–24).

developing countries.[3] Not surprisingly, there are several theories on this issue including the following[4]:

Proponents of the "divergence" perspective argue that cultural differences between societies such as those that have been identified by Hofstede and others make it difficult for Western management theories and practices to be effectively applied in non-Western societal cultures that are typically found in the developing world. Scholars holding this view also reject the notion of a universal theory of management on the grounds that cultural differences cannot be overcome.[5]

The "universal" perspective contrasts directly and sharply with the divergence perspective and holds that applicability of management theories and practices is not limited by culture and that certain similar management practices—universal practices—can be identified in organizations all around the world regardless of the level of economic development in the location where they are operating.[6]

The "convergence" perspective argues that applicability of management theories is correlated with the level of economic development and industrialization of a society and that the adoption of Western-style management theories by developing countries is a function of their ability

---

[3] Hoskisson, R., L. Eden, C. Ming Lau, and M. Wright. 2000. "Strategy in Emerging Economies." *Academy of Management Journal* 43, no. 3, pp. 249–67.

[4] Derived from Hafsi, T., and M. Farashahi. *October 1, 2005*. "Applicability of Management Theories to Developing Countries: A Synthesis." *The Free Library* http://thefreelibrary.com/Applicability of management theories to developing countries: a...-a0141092760

[5] See Hofstede, G. 1994. "Cultural Constraints in Management Theories." *International Review of Strategic Management* 5, pp. 27–49; Jaeger, A. 1990. "The Applicability of Western Management Techniques in Developing Countries: A Cultural Perspective." In *Management in Developing Countries*, eds. A. Jaeger and R. Kanungo, London: Routlege, pp. 131–45.

[6] See Mintzberg, H. 1973. *The Nature of Managerial Work*. New York, NY: Harper & Row; Mintzberg, H. July-August 1975. "The Manager's Job--Folklore and Fact." *Harvard Business Review* 53, no. 4, p. 49; and Lubatkin, M., M. Ndiaye, and R. Vengroff. 1997. "The Nature of Managerial Work in Developing Countries: A Limited Test of the Universalist Hypothesis." *Journal of International Business Studies* 28, no. 4, pp. 711–33.

to overcome technical and economic difficulties rather than cultural constraints.

The "situational" or "contingency" theory dismisses the claims of the proponents of the universal perspective and argues that applicability of management theories will depend on situational factors such as the personality of the manager, the ownership structure of the firm, hierarchy, and whether the firm is privately or publicly owned and operated.

One of the earliest formal studies of the applicability of Western-style management theories to developing countries was conducted by Kiggundu et al. in the early 1980s and they concluded that those theories would only be applicable in situations where the organization in the developing country could behave as a closed system. In other words, when the theories related only to the core technology of an organization without reference to its external environment the theories tended to be applicable with conditions and results similar to those of organizations in developed countries; however, the theories would not be applicable in situations involving the external environment.[7]

In the decades following the publication of the Kiggundu et al. study, a growing number of researchers turned their attention to empirically studying the effectiveness of attempts to introduce and implement Western managerial practices in developing countries. For example, Wood and Caldas conducted extensive research on the successes and failures associated with attempts to adopt imported managerial expertise into Brazil.[8] They posited a model, or framework, for understanding the integration of foreign managerial techniques in Brazil that began with various external,

---

[7] Hafsi, T., and M. Farashahi. *October 1, 2005.* "Applicability of Management Theories to Developing Countries: A Synthesis." *The Free Library* http://thefreelibrary.com/Applicability of management theories to developing countries: a...-a0141092760

[8] See Wood, T., and M. Caldas. 2002. "Adopting Imported Managerial Expertise in Developing Countries: The Brazilian Experience." *Academy of Management Executive* 16, no. 2, pp. 18–32. The description of Brazilian experiences with ISO 9000, reengineering and enterprise resource planning in the following paragraph is adapted from a discussion on page 19 of the cited article. See also Caldas, M., and T. Wood. 1997. "'For the English to See': The Importation of Managerial Technology in Late 20th Century Brazil." *Organization* 4, no. 4, pp. 517–34.

or contextual, factors such as the historical roots and cultural heritage of the country, particularly "plasticity" and "formalism"; contemporary external influences, including globalization and the sudden need for Brazil to transition from a feudal, agrarian economy into a player on the world economic stage; and low national competitiveness due to protectionist policies and underdeveloped productivity tools. Wood and Caldas emphasized that the two cultural traits—"plasticity" and "formalism"— significantly influenced the receptivity of Brazilians to foreign managerial techniques. On the one hand, plasticity, or an "openness and permeability to foreign influences," triggered an apparent acceptance of foreign items; however, the formalism in Brazilian societal culture meant there was a "tendency to adopt façade behaviors resulting in a discrepancy between the formal and the real," including behavior designed to deceive foreigners that alien practices were being adopted when, in fact, they were being resisted or only being partially adopted.[9] The framework also included intermediate factors, including diffusion agents (e.g., Brazilian government and its agencies, business schools, business media, and consultancies), that drove the promotion, dissemination, and legitimization of new ideas. For example, Caldas and Wood noted that initiatives to adopt imported managerial practices such as the ISO 9000 system were often driven by government programs that provided incentives to firms if they pursued ISO certification.[10]

Caldas and Wood found evidence that Brazilian managers perceived programs and projects based on ISO certification to be irrelevant and/ or inappropriate and that efforts to develop ISO systems actually raised costs and contributed to organizational rigidity because the conditions that existed in Brazilian firms were not favorable to such systems (i.e., poorly skilled laborers, high power distance, and highly centralized decision-making processes). Reengineering programs launched in Brazil during the mid- and late-1990s also yielded minimal benefits, which Wood and Caldas blamed on a failure to take into account organizational

---

[9] Wood, T., and M. Caldas. 2002. "Adopting Imported Managerial Expertise in Developing Countries: The Brazilian Experience." *Academy of Management Executive* 16, no. 2, pp. 18–32, 22.

[10] Id. at 23.

culture, competencies, and strategies. Other unexpected and damaging consequences of reengineering in Brazil flowed from the tendency of firms to use the programs as an excuse for downsizing for its own sake, rather than enhancing productivity, and this led to "loss of leadership, deterioration of organizational climate, decrease of organizational memory, reduction of productivity and efficiency, decline of perceived product and/or service quality, and hammering of organizational reputation." Finally, while the introduction of enterprise resource planning did result in some improvements with respect to integration and quality of information, gains in productivity and competitiveness were rare due to scope and planning mistakes and failure to customize the new systems to the specific organizational needs of Brazilian firms.

Wood and Caldas concluded that Brazilian firms often appeared to adopt foreign managerial practices in response to political, institutional, and substantive pressures but that cultural factors, notably formalism, and contemporary economic and social factors, such as poorly skilled workers, led to unsuccessful and unreasoned adoption of the practices with little added value.[11] Wood and Caldas had also cited the "level of critical reasoning" as an important factor in predicting the success of effectively adopting foreign managerial techniques, noting that higher levels of critical reasoning would allow local managers to critically analyze the techniques and adapt them to local conditions in a way that would increase the changes of effective integration. Wood and Callas noted that the significant political and institutional pressures in Brazil to appear to adopt foreign methods quickly deprived local managers of the time or incentive to critically analyze the proposed solutions and the result was that "most adoptions tend to be uncritical, and the results for firms may be quite harmful."[12]

In 2005, Hafsi and Farashahi decided it was time to take a fresh look at the research that had been conducted since the Kiggundu et al. article and undertook a review of 170 articles that were published from 1983 through 2002 to test their hypothesis that, despite the findings of researchers such as Caldas and Wood, circumstances had changed and

---

[11] Id. at 21 and 25.
[12] Id. at 21.

that Western-based concepts of general management and organizational theories had achieved widespread applicability in developing countries.[13] Their review led them to conclude that the "[r]esearchers working on organizations in developing countries will find a managerial behaviour that is similar to what may be seen in the developed countries." Hafsi and Frashahi suggested that their conclusions could be traced to a mix of environmental changes since the early 1980s as well as to extension of organizational theory to cover an increasing variety of circumstances and organizations.[14] In their view, the key environmental changes included the following:

Major global political and economic institutions, such as the World Bank and the International Monetary Fund, imposed their structural adjustment framework on many emerging and developing economies.[15] While this has not necessarily produced the economic growth that was anticipated and desired, it has been successful from a process perspective and, as a result, local institutions—governments that insisted on continuous intervention in the economy and commercial markets—have been pushed aside and replaced by growing influence of global institutions dominated by Western countries.[16] While this has sometimes caused

---

[13] Hafsi, T., and M. Farashahi. *October 1, 2005.* "Applicability of Management Theories to Developing Countries: A Synthesis." *The Free Library* http://thefreelibrary.com/Applicability of management theories to developing countries: a...-a0141092760

[14] Farashahi, M., T. Hafsi, and R. Molz. 2005. "Institutionalized Norms of Conducting Research and Social Realities: A Research Synthesis of Empirical Works From 1983-2002." *International Journal of Management Reviews* 7, no. 1.

[15] Kamarck, A.M. 1996. "The World Bank: Challenges and Creative Responses." In *The Bretton Woods-GATT system: Retrospect and Prospect After Fifty Years*, ed. O. Kirshner, 106–27. London: M.E, Sharpe.; Knoop, C.I., and G.C. Lodge. 1996. "World Bank (A): Under Siege." *Harvard Business School Case*, 9–797. Boston: Harvard Business School Press.; Rich, B. 1994. *Mortgaging the Earth: The World Bank, Environmental Impoverishment, and the Crisis of Development.* Boston: Beacon Press; and Wapenhans, W. 1995. *What's Ahead For the World Bank?* Flint, MI: Charles Stewart Mott Foundation Publications.

[16] With regard to how interaction between local institutions and global ones have influenced regulators, firms and markets in developing countries, see Carney, M., and M. Farashahi. 2006. "Transnational Institutions in Developing Countries:

resentment in developing countries, it has also softened the view of Western management and organizational practices in those countries and they are now increasingly seen as being acceptable.[17]

A number of events and innovations have accelerated globalization of markets, industries, and firms including reduction of tariff and non-tariff barriers, creation of the World Trade Organization, and the emergence, growth, and maturation of large free trade areas (e.g., the European Union, ASEAN, and the North American Free Trade Agreement).[18]

Barriers to cross-border communication have been struck down by rapid and often astonishing technological innovations, thus facilitating the movement toward global uniformity of perceptions and understanding regarding fundamental financial and economic issues and potential solutions.[19]

Most emerging and developing countries have embraced and launched privatization programs and the processes and practices of privatization have become more uniform around the world.[20]

The rapid global growth of industries based on the application of common and complex technologies has pushed developing and emerging countries to learn and adopt the managerial rules, norms, and

---

The Case of Iranian Civil Aviation." *Organization Studies* 27, no. 1, pp. 53–77. In general, developing countries looking to build and enhance their own capabilities in a complex and technology-driven area such as commercial airlines must be prepared to recognize and follow global regulatory schemes and managerial, technical and security norms dictated by manufacturers and investors from Western countries.

[17] Lubatkin, M., M. Ndiaye, and R. Vengroff. 1997. "The Nature of Managerial Work in Developing Countries: A Limited Test of the Universalist Hypothesis." *Journal of International Business Studies* 28, no. 4, pp. 711–33.

[18] Doz, Y. 1990. *Strategic Management in Multinational Companies.* Oxford: Pergamon; and Porter, M. 1990. *The Competitive Advantage of Nations.* London: Macmillan.

[19] Eisenmann, T. 2003. "High Definition TV: The Grand Alliance." *Harvard Business School Case 9-804-*103, Boston: Harvard Business School Press; and Henderson, R., and D. Yoffie. 2004. "Nokia and MIT's project Oxygen." *Harvard Business School Case 9-704-474*, Boston: Harvard Business School Press.

[20] World Bank Group. 2003. Washington, D.C.: World Development Report, 1999-2003.

theories associated with those industries. This has been particularly true in instances where globalization has been led by multinational firms as has been the cases in industries such as banking and automobiles. The standardization that so often accompanies globalization has often clashed with strong local tastes and cultural constraints including religious practices; however, even in those instances multinational firms have generally found a way to make reasonable accommodations for local preferences while implementing managerial practices and administrative techniques that are quite similar in most parts of the world (e.g., automobile manufacturers use the same standards to manage production and train workers in every country where they build their products).

More and more firms headquartered in countries around the world have adopted and implemented global growth strategies that has resulted in wider and freer access to markets, capital, human resources, and other assets and facilitated the transfer of managerial theories through actual practice in developing and emerging countries.[21] Multinational firms, in particular, have taken the lead in introducing and popularizing effective management practices that other firms, including many in developing countries, want to emulate. The practice of multinational firms of entering into joint ventures and other strategic alliances with local partners in developing countries is another way in which these firms are leading the push toward convergence in management practices.[22]

Managing training has become more uniform and standardized around the world and developing countries in particular has experienced substantial growth in the number of formal management training programs and business schools sponsored and staffed by Western-based organizations such as the Association to Advance Collegiate Schools of

[21] Doz, Y. 1985. *Strategic Management in Multinational Companies.* Oxford: Pergamon; and Marnet, O. 2005. "Economic Governance in the Age of Globalization." *Journal of Economic Issues* 39, no. 1, pp. 282–85.

[22] See J. Lee, T. Roehl, and S. Choe. 2000. "What Makes Management Style Similar and Distinct Across Borders? Growth, Experience and Culture in Korean and Japanese Firms." *Journal of International Business Studies* 31, no. 4, pp. 631–52.

Business and the Association of MBAs.[23] The result has been that managers being trained today in developing countries are more likely to be exposed to, and adopt, techniques, behavioral norms, and values that are substantially similar to those being introduced to their colleagues in the United States and other Western countries.[24]

Hafsi and Farashahi argued that, taken together, the changes listed earlier had led to the development and dissemination of shared knowledge and technical language among managers around the world regardless of the level of development of the countries in which they are practicing. They also noted that the global environment for business activities had been transformed by advances in technology and elimination of trade barriers that allowed great mobility of capital, labor, and other resources and wider and freer access to markets around the world. In addition, Hafsi and Farashahi felt that these trends had reduced the traditional ability of governments in developing countries to exercise inordinate amounts of control over their local economies and had forced public officials in those countries to begin acting in the same way as their colleagues in the industrialized world and adopt policies, such as privatization, that turned responsibility for commerce and innovation over to managers in the private sector. In their words: "To restate the obvious, we claim that an important process of institutional diffusion has taken place in the last decades. It has been pushed by international agencies' regulatory processes; by powerful normative processes that have defined good economic practices and determined the behaviour of economists and managers all over the world; and by dominant cultural-cognitive processes whereby

---

[23] Venezia, G. 2005. "Impact of Globalization of Public Administration Practices on Hofstede's Cultural Indices." *Journal of American Academy of Business* 6, no. 2, p. 344.

[24] The spread of Western management techniques to developing countries has corresponded to the evolution of management toward more of a science than an art, a phenomenon which has led to global training practices supported by what Hafsi and Farashahi referred to as the "strong homogenizing effect of certification associations and agencies." See also Wright, P., and G. Geroy. 2003. "Is it Time for ISO-9000 Managers?" *Management Research News* 26, no. 1, pp. 41–54.

western civilization mostly economic values take over traditional values (citations omitted)."[25]

Impact of Emergence of Global Competitors from Developing Countries

Interest in management outside of the United States, Europe, Japan, and other Asian countries such as Korea was fueled by the emergence of new global competitors such as the so-called BRIC countries: Brazil, Russia, India, and China, and it is now increasingly common to see articles and books comparing management practices in those countries to those used in the United States and other developed countries. In many instances, however, the primary thread of inquiry is on how US-based management practices, particularly in the human resources area, can be transferred to these developing economies, often with the anticipation that US multinationals will be establishing a large presence in those countries and are interested in importing their own management techniques as opposed to learning and applying indigenous practices. Many developing countries have their own body of research on local management practices compiled and recorded by academics, consultants, and policy makers in those countries—India is a particularly good example of a developing country with a substantial body of indigenous management literature; however, these materials are often difficult to access and may not have been translated to make it useful for interested parties from outside those countries.

The dichotomy between developed and developing countries, and the members of each of those groups, has a long history and has become deeply engrained in the minds of many scholars, policy makers, and ordinary citizens around the world. However, there is evidence of significant changes, which, if taken to their seemingly logical conclusion, will disrupt orthodox thinking about the sources of best practices for managers and will generate new ideas among scholars researching management in

---

[25] Hafsi, T., and M. Farashahi. *October 1,* 2005. "Applicability of Management Theories to Developing Countries: A Synthesis." *The Free Library* http://thefreelibrary.com/Applicability of management theories to developing countries: a...-a0141092760

developing countries. Already we are seeing large enterprises from countries still classified as "developing," such as Brazil, China, and India, involved in battles to assume ownership and managerial control over valuable economic assets in industrialized countries—and sometimes the only serious bidders are firms from the developing countries. In addition, industrialized countries are seeing progressively higher levels of inbound foreign investment from developing countries, often accompanied by a transfer of managers and their own managerial styles and practices from the investing country. Observing these events, Punnett has commented:

> What literature there is on management interactions between developing and developed countries implicitly assumes that managers from developed countries will be adapting to the environment in developing countries. The reverse may be more and more the reality of the management challenges of the 21st century.[26]

Developing Countries as Testing Grounds for New Management Theories

There is no question that introduction and transfer of "foreign" management theories and practices into developing countries has been a long and challenging process that is far from ending and which has been complicated by various factors including the importance of history, values and unwritten rules, norms, and related practices that cannot be easily identified and understood by outsiders. However, globalization generally, as well as the specific factors emphasized by Hafsi and Frashahi, have become sources of change for values and institutions in developing countries and recent years have seen countries such as China, India, Korea, and Turkey willingly seek out and adapt various Western management practices in a way rarely thought to be possible in the past. As a result, Hafsi and Frashahi posited the somewhat radical suggestion that "the question, whether Western-based theoretical development is applicable to developing countries,

---

[26] Punnett, B. "Management in Developing Countries." http://cavehill-uwi. academia.edu/BettyJanePunnett/Papers/181413/Managing_in_Developing_ Countries

may have become irrelevant," and then went on to explain that if one does concede that Western management theories can be effectively applied in many ways in developing countries then it was time to include those countries as part of "normal" scientific development that simply expands the diversity of contexts and circumstances in which discoveries regarding organizational structures and management can be made.

Hafsi and Frashahi predicted that developing countries may, in the future, provide novel and interesting ideas for managers in more industrialized countries, particularly as managers in the United States and Western Europe struggle to compete in fast changing and relatively unstable environments that have long been the norm in developing countries. Hafsi and Farashahi noted: "What is discovered in organizations in Texas, France or Saudi Arabia may or may not apply to organizations in Bangladesh, California or the UK; but we can at least relate the reasons to well-known concepts and theories, in particular to developments that recognize the importance of perceptions, values, beliefs and other soft influences on decision-makers' behaviour."[27] What this means is that in order for organizational management theory and research to be robust, timely, and useful in the future it should include study of practices in all of the aforementioned geographical locations coupled with rejection of the historical notion of management practices in developing countries being a degraded, or poor, form of management.

A. de Waal also expressed high hopes for the value of management studies in developing countries and argued that it could reasonably be assumed that the "highly dynamic environment Î [in these countries] Î is a good testing ground for new theory, techniques and concepts of business and management."[28] He was more cautious than Hafsi and Frashahi about

---

[27] Hafsi, T., and M. Farashahi. *October 1, 2005.* "Applicability of Management Theories to Developing Countries: A Synthesis." *The Free Library* http://thefreelibrary.com/Applicability of management theories to developing countries: a...-a0141092760

[28] de Waal, A. 2007. "Is Performance Management Applicable in Developing Countries?: The Case of a Tanzanian College." *International Journal of Emerging Markets* 2, no. 1, pp. 63–83, 68. (citing Pacek, N., and D. Thorniley. 2004. *Emerging Markets, Lessons for Business Success and the Outlook for Different Markets.* London: The Economist).

the efficacy of Western management practices in emerging markets due to significant cultural differences, but pointed out that if such practices could not be easily transferred then it was imperative for management scholars all over the world to seek out new solutions to managerial issues that would suit the specific cultural, economic, and political conditions found in developing countries. It does appear that interest in this type of research is increasing with the initial work focusing primarily on topics such as human resources management, new public management, and management control and information systems.[29]

Challenges for Managers in Developing Countries

The environment for business activities in developing countries—economic, political, and social conditions—generally varies significantly from the environment confronting managers in developed countries and this imposes significant and unique challenges for managers in developing countries as they attempt to set and execute their operational plans and strategies for their enterprises. For example, managers in developing countries are typically faced with production difficulties, poor infrastructure conditions, market uncertainties and disruptions, unstable and turbulent macroeconomic conditions, financial restrictions, governmental controls, and unstable and underdeveloped political systems and institutions, inadequate access to reliable information, relatively primitive technology levels, and a lack of skilled and trained human capital. Managers in developing countries must also pay particular attention to the health and development of the natural resources sector in their countries since natural resources continue to play an important role in the economies of many of those countries as they embark on a transition toward

---

[29] Design and implementation of management accounting systems, for example, has been frequently studied by researchers. See, e.g., Anderson, S.W., and W. Lanen. 1999. "Economic Transition, Strategy and the Evolution of Management Accounting Practices: The Case of India." *Accounting, Organisations and Society* 24, nos. 5–6, pp. 379–412; and Waweru, N., Z. Hoque, and E. Uliana. 2004. "Management Accounting Change in South Africa, Case Studies from Retail Services." *Accounting, Auditing and Accountability Journal* 17, no. 5, pp. 675–704.

greater reliance on jobs and economic activities in the manufacturing and services sectors. In addition, the opportunities and pressures of globalization raise difficult and emotional issues of business ethics and corporate social responsibility. Finally, like managers all around the world, managers in developing countries must understand how elements of societal culture may impact the efficacy of the managerial practices and styles that they attempt to employ.

Management Processes in Developing Countries

Most of the popular models of managerial activities focus on certain key functions. In the early 2000s, Jones et al. referred to management as "the process of using an organization's resources to achieve specific goals through the functions of planning, organizing, leading and controlling"[30]; however, long before that Henri Fayol pioneered the notion of "functions of management" in his 1916 book *Administration Industrielle et Generale* in which he identified and described five functions of managers—planning, organizing, commanding, coordinating, and controlling—that he believed were universal and required of all managers as they went about performing their day-to-day activities regardless of whether they were operating in the business environment or overseeing the activities of governmental, military, religious, or philanthropic organizations. In 1937 Gulick and Urwick added two additional items to Fayol's original list: reporting and budgeting.[31] Other management theorists working and writing during the 1950s and 1960s also embraced what has become known as the "process school of management" based on the notion that management should be viewed as a linear process that included an identifiable set of several interdependent functions. For example, Koontz et al.

---

[30] Jones, G., J. George, and C. Hill. 2000. *Contemporary Management*, 2nd ed. New York, NY: Irwin/McGraw-Hill.

[31] Description derived from Unit 8 Classical Approach: Luther Gulick and Lyndall Urwick, http://egyankosh.ac.in/bitstream/123456789/25509/1/Unit-8.pdf The model proposed by Gulick and Urwick first appeared in Gulick, L., and L. Urwick., eds. 1937. Papers on the Science of Administration. New York, NY: Institute of Public Administration.

identified the following five activities as "major management functions": planning, organizing, staffing, directing, and controlling.[32]

While the process school of management, and the accompanying similar lists of five to seven managerial functions, has remained a dominant analytical framework, others have criticized this approach. Perhaps the most well-known opposition came from Mintzberg and his suggestion of an alternative descriptive model of the ten core "roles," or organized sets of behaviors, that could be identified with a managerial position. Mintzberg divided these roles into three groups: interpersonal roles (i.e., figure-head, leader, and liaison offer), informational roles (i.e., monitors, disseminators, spokespeople) and decisional roles (i.e., entrepreneurs, disturbance handlers, resource allocators, and negotiators).[33] Mintzberg's work generated a fair amount of debate regarding the validity of the process school of management since it questioned the linearity of managerial activities and suggested that the manager's life is more realistically viewed as a continuously changing set of roles that demanded different skills.

When studying management practices and styles in developing countries a threshold question is whether or not such a model of the management process, which was created by Western researchers working in largely developed and industrialized economies, is applicable and useful for understanding how managers operate in those countries. Punnett cautioned that the model had certain "Western biases" that must be accounted for when it is used for analysis of actions in developing countries. For example, she pointed out that "the process in the model is based on a sequential, logical, rational set of discrete activities" and also "assumes control over the environment so that making plans, designing structures, choosing people for specific jobs, and measuring outcomes are all reasonable activities." While all of this is consistent with a Western view of the world, Punnett argued that non-Western developing countries "do not see the world in the same straight, sequenced pattern" and that the efficacy of the model in those countries may be undermined by

---

[32] Koontz, H., C. O'Donnell, and H. Weihrich. 1970. *Management,* 7th ed. New York, NY: McGraw-Hill.

[33] See Mintzberg, H. July–August 1975. "The Manager's Job: Folklore and Fact." *Harvard Business Review* 53, no. 4, pp. 49–61.

different perspectives regarding time orientation and the role of fate and the degree of control that people actually have over their environment.[34] To the extent that there is truth in Punnett's words, which are supported by a good deal of empirical evidence on world views of managers and subordinates in many developing countries, it may well be that Mintzberg's family of roles would be a better reference point for developing country managers looking to identify the skills they might need to carry out the full scope of their jobs.

Models of the management process in various countries must also take into account the impact of societal culture. This is true regardless of whether countries are developed and industrialized or developing. Generalizing about the profile of societal cultures for developing countries is difficult and problematic; however, it is probably fair to say that the cultural characteristics of many developing countries differ from those found in the United States and other industrialized Western countries and these differences will be reflected in how managers in developed countries approach activities such as planning, leading, and controlling. Punnett observed that "[d]eveloping countries have generally been found to be somewhat more collective than developed countries, somewhat more accepting of power differentials, somewhat more averse to uncertainty, and more fatalistic." She also noted that in developing countries the "need for achievement" was generally lower and gender roles were more firmly delineated, a situation that often led to discrimination against women with respect to property rights (e.g., land ownership and inheritance rights), educational opportunities, and income.[35]

Punnett argued that the collection of societal culture characteristics described earlier tended to push managers in developing countries toward a "Theory X" management style that featured rigid hierarchies; direction from the top down, albeit with modest levels of input from subordinates and a touch of paternalism and parental benevolence; and tight controls and rare challenges to managerial instructions by subordinates. Punnett

---

[34] Punnett, B. r.d. "Management in Developing Countries." http://cavehill-uwi.academia.edu/BettyJanePunnett/Papers/181413/Managing_in_Developing_Countries

[35] Id.

suggested that the cultural context in developing countries raised serious questions about how managers in those countries should approach the most commonly mentioned managerial functions and activities. For example, she questioned whether planning really necessary if events are predetermined, what good were organizational charts if power and responsibilities are based on personal influence and relationships, and were control systems irrelevant when subordinates are culturally conditioned to unquestionably act upon the instructions of their superiors?

In attempting to explain the foundation for the characteristics of societal culture in developing countries and attitudes in those countries toward various business-related activities, Punnett and others have emphasized the impact of the long periods of colonial occupation by European countries, many of which continue to play a strong role in the political and economic affairs of their former colonies even after independence. Punnett noted that the colonies were in subordinate positions in relation to their "colonial masters" from Europe and thus were dependent on European officials with respect to a wide array of decisions relating to politics, economic, and business. She suggested that this dependence has survived in the form of a lingering tendency among Africans to look to others for decisions and to unquestionably accept those decisions when they come from persons perceived to have legitimate authority in African culture. Remnants of the "top down" colonial authority structure, with little input from the local level, can also be found in the high power distance and tall organizational hierarchies that remain prevalent in post-independence African businesses. Another interesting observation is that the relative lack of marketing acumen among African businesses can be traced to the fact that colonies were generally exclusive producers for their overlords and thus there was no need to develop skills in business-related functions outside of production.[36]

Many continue to believe that Western models of managerial functions and activities may not be totally applicable to developing countries and the study of managerial processes in developing countries must certainly take into account the unique challenges confronting managers in

---

[36] Id.

those countries. However, in spite of those limitations, managerial processes in developing countries are often discussed by reference to dimensions familiar to scholars from the West: planning, organizing, staffing,
leading, and coordinating. Whether or not these dimensions are "universal" remains a matter for debate.[37] Moreover, even if one can reasonably
assume that managers in developing countries must devote some amount
of their time and resources to planning, coordinating, and other activities
previously listed, they will necessarily bring a different perspective to due
to factors such as societal culture, the level of training of their subordinates, their own prior exposure to managerial training and technology,
and, finally, the local institutional influences on business activities (i.e.,
national business systems). For example, Farashahi suggested that managers in developing countries have less sensitivity, or sometimes even no
response, to competition and economic objectives given the reality that
firms in developing countries remain so dependent on central governments that strictly control the allocation of resources and dictate plans to
both public and private sector enterprises.[38] Farashashi also suggested that
managers in developing countries are very sensitive to social relations and
political objectives, which may impact staffing policies and decisions, and
that they are less used to making and implementing decisions.

Management Training in Developing Countries

Managers in all parts of the world, including developing countries, can
be expected to be most effective when they possess certain fundamental skills—technical, human, conceptual and design—that are necessary and appropriate for their particular managerial level and scope of
responsibilities It is reasonable and useful to think of managerial training
in developing countries as having the important objective of building
"management capacity" in those countries, both at the national level and

---

[37] See, e.g., Lubatkin, M.H., M. Ndiaye, and R. Vengroff. 1997. "The Nature
of Managerial Work in Developing Countries: A Limited Test of the Universalist
Hypothesis." *Journal of International Business Studies* 28, no. 4, pp. 711–33.
[38] Farashahi, M. "Management Systems in Developing Countries." http://sba.
muohio.edu/abas/1999/farashme.pdf

within specific enterprises. A useful definition of management capacity has been provided by the European Commission, albeit in a different context: research and policy advice regarding support for the creation and growth of small and medium-sized enterprises (SMEs) in the European Union. In a report on "management capacity building," the European Commission noted that "management capacity building has been understood broadly as encompassing all the means through which a startup enterprise or an existing SME gathers and strengthens its knowledge and competencies in four main areas having an impact on a firm's profitability: (1) strategic and management knowledge aspects (including human resource management, accounting, financing, marketing, strategy, and organizational issues, such as production and information and technology aspects); (2) understanding the running of the business and of the potential opportunities or threats (including visions for further development of activities, current and prospective marketing aspects); (3) willingness to question and maybe review the established patterns (innovation, organizational aspects); and (4) attitudes toward investing time in management development or other needed competencies."[39] The report also identified three main categories of means that can be used to acquire the needed managerial skills, including training, advice from professionals and/or consultants, and "knowledge sharing" activities, such as networking and Internet research, aimed at finding out applicable information.[40]

Training and skills building programs have frequently been offered in developing countries through international aid organizations, and it has been observed that "training constitutes an important part of both developing country budgets and overseas development assistance."[41] In fact, international organizations have invested significant amounts in various types of "technical cooperation," which includes training, equipment,

---

[39] European Commission. September 2006. "Final Report of the Expert Group on Building Management Capacity." *Brussels: Directorate-General for Enterprise and Industry of the European Commission*, p. 6.

[40] Id.

[41] Nelson, M. February 2006. *Does Training Work? Re-Examining Donor-Sponsored Training Programs in Developing Countries*. World Bank Institute: Capacity Development Briefs.

and advice. Unfortunately, methodological and data problems have made it difficult to accurately compute the "return" on these investments and "most evaluations of training in a development context is that it has proved less effective than expected."[42]

While work needs to be done on uncovering and analyzing empirical evidence, there is a general impression that a handful of "favorable conditions" need to be present in order for training and skills building programs in developing countries to be effective. For example, it is recommended that "capacity development Î be integrated in a country-led development strategy,"[43] which means avoiding one-off training events and minimizing activities that primarily benefit individuals and focusing on initiatives that can support needed institutional and organizational changes. In addition, to the extent possible training programs should be designed and implemented in ways that do not get caught up in local politics. In many cases, donor countries create and use training programs as a way to favor and support their own institutes, universities, and consultants. For their part, governments in developing countries often hand out opportunities to participate in training junkets as political favors. In that same vein, it is recommended that the organizations in developing countries benefitting from the training take ownership of the results of the programs, thus providing incentives for those organizations to take the programs seriously and commit their most valuable resources (i.e., people, time, and capital) to making sure that the programs are effective and successful. Finally, both sides of the training equation—donors and recipients—must commit to setting benchmarks for success before the programs begin and continuously measuring performance toward those benchmarks once the training has been delivered.[44]

Improvement of local business education institutions has also been a priority among efforts to enhance capacity building in developing countries. For example, the Global Business School Network (GBSN) is an international non-profit organization focusing on the improvement of management education in emerging markets. The GBSN has undertaken

---

[42] Id.

[43] Id.

[44] Id.

a number of initiatives to build competencies within business schools in developing countries including strengthening and expanding existing curricula; facilitating faculty training, mentoring, and developing; creating entrepreneurship modules; researching, writing, and disseminating local case studies and other instructional materials; and creating networks for the dissemination of knowledge, best practices, and "lessons learned." In addition, the GBSN acts as a hub for connecting program schools in developing countries with organizational partners, including business schools in developed countries, to foster communication and the flow of resources to the program schools. For further discussion, see the GBSN website. In addition, the World Federal of Engineers, a nongovernmental international organization that brings together national engineering organizations from over 90 nations and represents some 8,000,000 engineers from around the world, has led several programs designed to improve engineering education and practice in developing countries.[45]

Training through business education at universities and colleges in developing countries is an important topic and there are various issues that often must be addressed simultaneously and on an ongoing basis as the needs of developing countries change and evolve. In many cases, business schools in developing countries begin by imitating the curriculum offered in the United States and other developed countries; however, it soon becomes apparent that modifications are needed to meet the needs of the local communities. Accounting and finance are fundamental subjects for developing countries as they transition toward market-oriented economies and the curriculum must also address marketing, particularly international marketing of consumer products, planning, and distribution. While training for "general manager" positions is needed in developing countries there is a rapidly increasing need for development of specialists such as professional marketers, project managers, and controllers. The "demand" for certain skills varies from country-to-country. For example, students in many countries need more coursework in computer skills,

---

[45] Jones, R. "Engineering Capacity Building in Developing Countries." http://worldexpertise.com/Engineering_Capacity_Building_in_Developing_Countries.htm

oral communications and foreign language, and leadership and interpersonal communications skills. Other issues of interest include the creating and offering of advanced degrees, such as MBAs; incorporating distance learning techniques, particularly in larger countries where it is difficult for all students to travel to a central training hub; providing education to local instructors on how to teach the new business topics; building research capacity to support the expansion of specific scholarly work on management in developing countries; and, finally, academic–industry collaboration to improve worker skills and transfer scientific knowledge and technology from the university laboratory to the factory floor.[46]

Additional research on management skills acquisition in developing countries has focused on knowledge transfer methods and the ability of developing countries to retain qualified managers once they have been trained, either locally or overseas. For example, Beudry and Francois suggested that continuously observing other competent managers ("learning by seeing") may actually be a more effective means for acquisition of managerial skills than the traditional "learning by doing" that emphasizes repetitive practice of new skills.[47] The same researchers also cautioned that hopes that managers sent abroad for training would return home to help disseminate their knowledge locally and support development might be misplaced. Specifically, they observed that "the incentive for managers to migrate from a more developed country (where managerial knowledge is

---

[46] For an interesting series of essays on business and management education in developing countries around the world, see McIntyre, J.R., and I. Alon., eds. 2005. *Business and Management Education in Transitioning and Developing Countries*. Armonk, NY: M.E. Sharpe.

[47] Beudry, P., and P. Francois. 2010. "Managerial Skills Acquisition and the Theory of Economic Development." *Review of Economic Studies* 77, no. 1, pp. 90–126. Beudry and Francois explained that "'learning by seeing' is a process whereby, when working as an unskilled worker in production, some of the knowledge that is currently only held by a worker's skilled counterparts is transmitted to the work through experience Î [b]y working alongside (or as a subordinate to) the skilled, unskilled workers can succeed in picking up the skills required to fill skilled positions in the firm, or use that experience to themselves startup firms of their own that will replicate the product methods that they have learned."

abundant) to a less developed country (where it is scarce) is Î very weak and possibly non-existent" an observation that they noted "has the potential to help understand the persistence of under-development."[48]

---

[48] Beudry, P., and P. Francois. 2005. "Managerial Skills Acquisition and the Theory of Economic Development." *Review of Economic Studies* 77, no. 1, pp. 90–126.

About the Author

Dr. Alan S. Gutterman is the founding director of the Sustainable Entrepreneurship Project (www.seproject.org). In addition, Alan's prolific output of practical guidance and tools for legal and financial professionals, managers, entrepreneurs, and investors has made him one of the best-selling individual authors in the global legal publishing marketplace. His cornerstone work, *Business Transactions Solution*, is on online-only product available and featured on Thomson Reuters' Westlaw, the world's largest legal content platform, which includes almost 200 book-length modules covering the entire life cycle of a business. Alan has also authored or edited over 70 books on sustainable entrepreneurship, management, business law and transactions, international law business and technology management for a number of publishers including Thomson Reuters, Kluwer, Aspatore, Oxford, Quorum, ABA Press, Aspen, Sweet & Maxwell, Euromoney, Business Expert Press, Harvard Business Publishing, CCH, and BNA. Alan has over three decades of experience as a partner and senior counsel with internationally recognized law firms counseling small and large business enterprises in the areas of general corporate and securities matters, venture capital, mergers and acquisitions, international law and transactions, strategic business alliances, technology transfers and intellectual property, and has also held senior management positions with several technology-based businesses including service as the chief legal officer of a leading international distributor of IT products headquartered in Silicon Valley and as the chief operating officer of an emerging broadband media company. He has been an adjunct faculty member at several colleges and universities, including Boalt Hall, Golden Gate University, Hastings College of Law, Santa Clara University, and the University of San Francisco, teaching classes on a diverse range of topics including corporate finance, venture capital, corporate law, Japanese business law and law and economic development, He received his AB, MBA, and JD from the University of California at Berkeley, a DBA from Golden Gate University, and a PhD from the University of Cambridge. For more information about Alan and his activities, please contact him directly at alangutterman@gmail.com, follow him on LinkedIn (https://www.linkedin.com/in/alangutterman/) and visit his website at alangutterman.com, which includes an extensive collection of links to his books and other publications and resource materials for students and practitioners of sustainable entrepreneurship.

Index

OTHER TITLES IN THE HUMAN RESOURCE MANAGEMENT AND ORGANIZATIONAL BEHAVIOR COLLECTION

- *Conflict First Aid: How to Stop Personality Clashes and Disputes from Damaging You or Your Organization* by Nancy Radford
- *How to Manage Your Career: The Power of Mindset in Fostering Success* by Kelly Swingler
- *Deconstructing Management Maxims, Volume I: A Critical Examination of Conventional Business Wisdom* by Kevin Wayne
- *Deconstructing Management Maxims, Volume II: A Critical Examination of Conventional Business Wisdom* by Kevin Wayne
- *The Real Me: Find and Express Your Authentic Self* by Mark Eyre
- *Across the Spectrum: What Color Are You?* by Stephen Elkins-Jarrett
- *The Human Resource Professional's Guide to Change Management: Practical Tools and Techniques to Enact Meaningful and Lasting Organizational Change* by Melanie J. Peacock
- *Tough Calls: How to Move Beyond Indecision and Good Intentions* by Linda D. Henman
- *The 360 Degree CEO: Generating Profits While Leading and Living with Passion and Principles* by Lorraine A. Moore
- *The Concise Coaching Handbook: How to Coach Yourself and Others to Get Business Results* by Elizabeth Dickinson

Announcing the Business Expert Press Digital Library

Concise e-books business students need for classroom and research

This book can also be purchased in an e-book collection by your library as

- a one-time purchase,
- that is owned forever,
- allows for simultaneous readers,
- has no restrictions on printing, and
- can be downloaded as PDFs from within the library community.

Our digital library collections are a great solution to beat the rising cost of textbooks. E-books can be loaded into their course management systems or onto students' e-book readers.
The **Business Expert Press** digital libraries are very affordable, with no obligation to buy in future years. For more information, please visit **www.businessexpertpress.com/librarians**. To set up a trial in the United States, please email **sales@businessexpertpress.com**.

www.ingramcontent.com/pod-product-compliance
Lightning Source LLC
Chambersburg PA
CBHW061316220326
41599CB00026B/4910